S L I G O
Land of Yeats' Desire

John Cowell

THE O'BRIEN PRESS
DUBLIN

One of Charles Bianconi's (1786-1875) 'long cars'.

Its History, Literature

W.B. Yeats, aged about seven months, with his nurse in Sligo.

Folklore & Landscapes

First published 1989 by The O'Brien Press
20 Victoria Road, Rathgar, Dublin 6, Ireland.
Published in paperback 1990.

British Library Cataloguing in Publication Data
Cowell, John, 1912 -
Land of yeats' desire: Sligo: its history,
literature, folklore & landscape.
1. Sligo (County), History
I. Title
941.7'2
ISBN 0-86278-186-8 hardback
ISBN0-86278-185-X paperback

10 9 8 7 6 5 4 3 2 1

Cover paintings: *Front* 'Ben Bulben' by T.P. Flanagan; *Back* 'The Old Pilot House, Rosses Point'
by Jack B. Yeats. Both pictures courtesy Noeleen and Vincent Ferguson.

Acknowledgements (photographs)
The author and publisher thank the following for photographs used in the book: Pat Duffy *page* 121; the National
Library 4, 5, 81 (t. and b.), 82, 84, 85, 87, 90, 91, 107 (t. and b.), 118, 171; Commissioners of Public Works 15, 128
(b.) 135, 145, 156, 166 (b.), 168; Noel and Briga Murphy 18, 132, 159, 174; Jim Eccles 22, 105, 106, 113, 114, 115,
165, 175; Sligo County Library 41, 45, 56, 98, 99, 102, 103, 111; Bord Failte 76, 124, 125 (b.), 129, 134 (b.), 138,
139, 161 (t. and b.), 162, 164, 169, 170, 180; Alfred Carroll, courtesy Fr J. Carroll 79, 100 (b.), 116, 134 (t.), 154;
Kevin and Peg Murray 123, 137, 183; George Gmelch 166 (t.); Tadhg Kilgannon 59, 75; Cambridge University 2,
21, 49; *Picture Post* (1948) 185 (t.); *The Irish Times* (1948) 185 (b.); *Times Pictorial* (1948) 186; *Illustrated* (1948)
187; drawings from the Wakeman collection 1, 3, 17 (t. and b.), 33, 100 (t.), 125 (t.), 128 (t.), 145 (t.), 146, 148, 153,
178. Every effort has been made to trace copyright holders; if, however, any oversight has occurred the holders of
such copyright should contact the publisher.

Extracts quoted courtesy A.P. Watt Ltd., on behalf of Michael B. Yeats and Macmillan, London, Ltd.

*Captions for pictures pages 1, 2, 3: Castle Dargan, drawn by W.F. Wakeman; Ben Bulben from the
air; cromlech at Carrowmore, W.F. Wakeman.*

Typeset at The O'Brien Press
Cover design: The Graphiconies
Book design: Michael O'Brien and Ide ní Laoghaire
Maps: Adrian Slattery
Printing: Betaprint International Ltd., Dublin

Contents

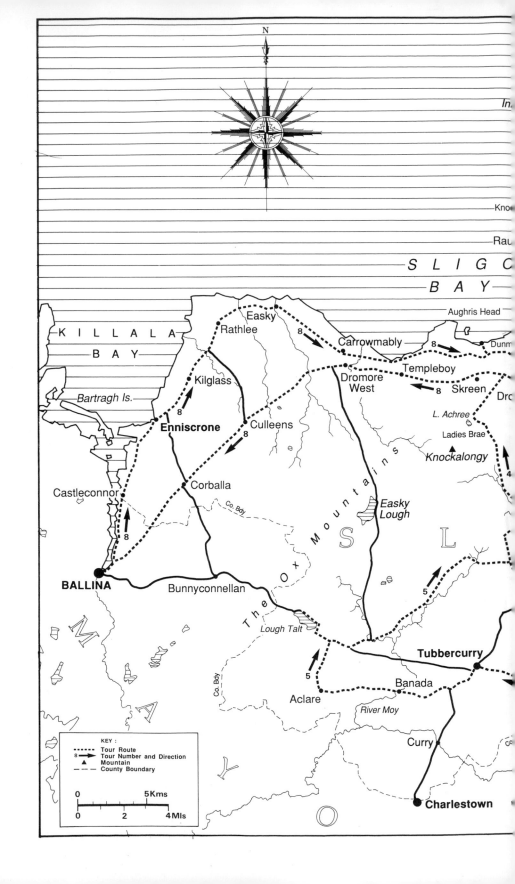

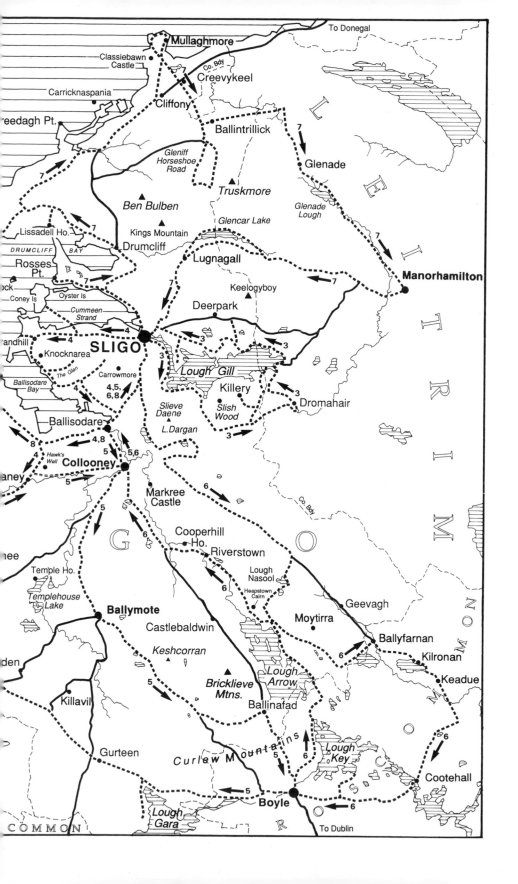

Preface

Over the years I have introduced many foreigners, and even Irish friends to the attractions of County Sligo. Too often the reaction has been one of surprise. They didn't know; they'd never heard; nobody had told them. Was it over-modesty, or an inexplicable taciturnity that prevented the people of Sligo from bruiting about the natural gifts that a generous God had specially chosen for them? For instance, who was it who decided to call Lough Gill 'The Killarney of the West', when Lough Gill was Lough Gill, with its own characteristic charms ever since time began? It is like nowhere else in this world. It is incomparable, like so much else throughout the Sligo countryside. If I make my point a little forcefully, that is because Sligo is my hereditary home, and one can never escape a jealous pride in the place that cast the spell of childhood's dreams.

Thankfully, Sligo has in the meantime, taken a more rightful place as one of the most beautiful regions in Ireland. Many factors have contributed to making it better known. But more than anything else it owes its growing reputation to the work of the poet Yeats, whose name is now synonymous with Sligo. He has enshrined the region for all time within the pages of English literature.

This book is not a history of Sligo, nor even a geography. It is a sort of salmagundi - a dish with sufficiently interesting ingredients to tempt the tourist in transit as well as to initiate the serious student into reading more widely. Of course there are those better qualified to write about Sligo, but until they do, my hope is that my book may help to bring the knowledge of its special charms to countless more than any one man could ever hope to introduce in person.

In the preparation of this book, and particularly in the discovery and provision of its illustrations, some of rare antiquity, with my publishers I am most grateful to the people of Sligo for their interest and for their unstinted help. In particular we must thank John McTernan, County Librarian, for his assistance in making available the W.F. Wakeman drawings done in 1879-80 for the Cooper family of Markree Castle and later presented by them to the Sligo County Library.

I acknowledge my gratitude to Michael O'Brien and to his staff for their work, often carried far into the night: Ide ní Laoghaire, Mairéad FitzGerald, Liz Meldon and Ivan O'Brien.

A TURBULENT HISTORY

Chapter I

The Beginnings

GHOSTS AND GOBLINS

To have grown up in an enchanted land was a privilege so rare, it seemed to put one among God's chosen. But that realisation dawned only with the years. As a small boy beauty was all about me. I saw it and loved it before I could understand it, before I could even spell the word.

My father, a country doctor, had come back from London to his native County Sligo, attracted by the shooting and fishing. His English wife had reservations, though in time the Skreen countryside captured her heart too. At first she measured our primitive isolation by telling her English friends and relatives that we lived thirteen miles from the nearest railway station. That was true enough, God knows, and thirteen miles in a blinding rainstorm in a tub-trap or on the wind-swept heights of a side-car could be a dampening experience. All this, of course, was before the First World War, and long before Yeats had put the corpus of his work between hardbacks, eventually to commercialise County Sligo as the Yeats Country.

Looking back I mostly remember sunshine. On a hill behind our house there was a rath. My mother called it a fort. It was my spiritual home, though I couldn't have recognised that at the time. An only boy, there I spent long, lonely hours savouring the all-round panorama, from Ben Bulben to the castle of Dromore, until every hill and hollow was imprinted on my mind for all time. There I read my first grown-up books: *Robinson Crusoe*, *Red Cloud*, *The Last Days of Pompeii*. There I first experienced the painful allure of distant horizons, the sadness of a day's end, the sun sinking into the Atlantic leaving a golden road to Greenland; there I watched the rising of a harvest moon, a huge scarlet orb hanging in the night sky over Queen Maeve's tomb on Knocknarea. Like Shaw on Dalkey Hill, it was high on my special rath in County Sligo that I first sensed 'the dreaming, the torturing, heart-scalding, never satisfying dreaming.'

My rath, of course, was haunted. Not by ordinary ghosts, but by the wicked fairies. Our maid told me I'd be whipped away some day as a changeling, and be substituted by a fairy child. Such information only served to lend the place a new sense of adventure. I never managed to see the little people, nor even hear their music, but I did find what I took to be their paths. Our maid's brother told me they were only rabbit-tracks, and I'd have to visit the rath at night if I wanted to see the fairies at work. That was more than I ever dared, for if I remember the sunshine of a Sligo childhood, I also remember the terrors of its dark. What with the ever-present supernatural, the horrors of our local wars, and child psychology a subject still in the future, the wonder is that so many of us reached adulthood still in a reasonable state of sanity.

'Sligo for a small boy was a fascinating place.' So said Bertie Smyllie, a late and legendary editor of *The Irish Times*. Fascinating was an under-statement, but then Smyllie was a towny. He grew up on the Mail Coach Road where there were street lights and traffic to banish the ghosts. It was different in the heart of the country.

Skreen is halfway between Sligo and Ballina. To the south rears Knocka-longy, the highest peak in the Ox Mountains. To the north is Sligo Bay and the broad Atlantic, whose moods can change within the hour, from blue tranquillity to green and towering terror. On the far horizon, in County Donegal, Slieve League, the highest sea-cliff in Europe, rises steeply to two thousand feet - 'that ocean mountain steep' as William Allingham, the Ballyshannon poet called it, 'six hundred yards in air aloft, six hundred in the deep'. In its panoramic grandeur, Skreen is but a microcosm of the whole enchanted county of Sligo.

Being a country lad had distinct advantages in a land full of adventure. Your imagination could run riot, urged to its extremities by the torrid tales of a wistfully naive people. You grew hungry for more and more of the same, and the darker the night, the greater the *frisson*, particularly if you had to pass a graveyard to get home. You hated to admit it, but terror of the dark took you by the throat, and you swore by the Almighty never again to listen to such poppycock.

But was it poppycock? Surely there must be a thread of reality somewhere, an underlying germ of truth? At any rate, you became as absorbed in listening as were the story-tellers in the telling, for every twist of the road home, every rath and gateway, every ivy-smothered ruin, had its own tenantry of hobgob-lins, fairy hosts, or sad and silent ghosts - all of them attractively repellent to a frightened boy wishful to be a man.

Of course, next morning with the daylight, when the sun dappled the mountains with swiftly-moving blobs of peacock blue, and the sea reflected the wispy clouds in a high-flying mackerelled sky, life was all bravado again. You could explore that ivy-smothered ruin, every stone of it, for reassurance.

12

John Cowell (behind) as a young boy, with his mother and sisters Vera, Tony and Bunty in Sligo, shortly after his father's death.

You satisfied yourself of the absurdity of those tales - but only temporarily. No amount of day-lit exploration could wipe out the night-time terror of the unknown.

With their telling and re-telling, ghost stories of the long-ago became familiar, and their dramatis personae almost acceptable. During the Troubled Times however, one's young blood really curdled, for the ghost stories were suddenly up-dated. Local lads recently shot dead were said to be seen walking the roads at night. These were people one remembered in life. The idea was hideous and horrifying, yet these tales were told in all sincerity by people whose commonsense I had otherwise no reason to doubt.

It was the coming of rural electrification, telephones and television that finally laid the ghosts for all time. Today's Sligonians, urban and rural, would laugh at the tales that terrified my generation. The carry-on in the soap operas and the soundlessly galloping horses of the headless coachman of Lugawarry have nothing in common but their banality. Of course, the preoccupation of their grandfathers and great-grandfathers with the occult had its origins in the history and pre-history in which County Sligo is immersed.

Before the tractor, the horse and cart were every farmer's lifeline. Here is our neighbour Mikey with Dolly, setting out for the bog for a load of peat, called 'turf' in County Sligo.

Stephen Rynne, the Kildare writer, had a theory that since the scholars took history out of the hands of the simple traditionalists, we no longer know anything for certain. Romantically speaking, he has a point. But about Sligo, this much we do know for certain: the town originated at an important ford on the Garavogue, the two-mile-long river that drains Lough Gill into the sea. The ford was the scene of many a battle. Strategically placed, it was where the Northmen crossed when they came south round the snout of Ben Bulben on a cattle-raid. And by it they retreated when the Connaughtmen beat them back into their northern fastnesses. Today the route is roughly the same - without the stepping stones.

FROM MOYTIRRA TO CARROWMORE

The early Christian monks tried to provide Ireland with a respectably historical past as ancient as that of Babylon, Egypt, Greece or Rome. The result was the *Lebor Gabhála*, a compilation recording the mythical invasions from the time of Adam. An early visitor was Nemedius, said to be eleventh in descent from Noah. We're told he arrived in Sligo and settled with his followers at Maugherow near Lissadell. Enjoyment by the Nemedians of Sligo's green and fertile land was rudely disturbed by the arrival of the Fomorians, whose way

14

Mythology claims Moytirra, with its dolmens, cairns and pillar-stones, as the site of the battle in which the Tuatha dé Danann routed the Firbolgs.

of life was piracy and plunder. These ruffians hadn't even established themselves when the Firbolgs landed in Mayo and overspread County Sligo. Later the Tuatha de Danaan landed on the Sligo coast, and with every intention of remaining, burnt their shipping. Efforts were made at power-sharing, like halving the country, but it was soon apparent that trouble was brewing, for both the invaded and the invaders were men of steely character.

The word Firbolg translates as Bagmen. Duald Mac Firbis, the seventeenth century Sligo genealogist, characterised the Firbolgs as a black-haired people, thieving, churlish, mean and contemptible, while the Tuatha de Danaan were fair-haired plunderers, large and vengeful. A challenge to fight was inevitable. It was King Eochy of the Firbolgs who issued it to King Nuada of the Tuatha some 2,000 years before Christianity and 700 years before the Siege of Troy.

Some commentators, like Sir William Wilde, believed the four-day battle took place at Moytura (the plain of the towers) near Cong in County Mayo. There he plotted the scene to his satisfaction. As if to confirm his belief, he also built a holiday home which he called Moytura House. But Sir William wasn't quite right. The true site - as far as myth can ever be true - of the Firbolg-de Danaan massacre in which, myth also has it, one hundred thousand

15

men fought, is at Moytirra near Highwood, above Kilmactranny in County Sligo.

Moytirra is a seven hundred feet high, grave-strewn, inhospitably desolate plateau one mile square, with valleys on three sides and Lough Arrow on its west. It is a weird and haunted place with a sense of doom about it. There are tower-like pillars, monoliths and obelisks scattered about, each weighing many tons.

The Firbolgs were favourites for the fight, for they had a unique general called Balor of the Evil Eye. As a child he had peeped in where druids were brewing a magic concoction. When the lid of the cauldron was lifted, escaping vapour carried the deadly venom of the brew into his single eye, situated in the middle of his forehead. As a result, Balor could strike whole armies dead with the terrible power of his cyclopian gaze. What happened at Moytirra isn't clear. Balor must have had an off-day, for the Tuatha de Danaan put King Eochy and the Firbolgs to flight. They overtook and killed the king on Beltra Strand (Traigh Eothuile), near Ballisodare, County Sligo. A cairn was raised over him, but time and the tides have erased it.

A profusion of little hills and valleys gives the lowlands of County Sligo a pleasant undulating appearance. This is because the area falls within the Drumlin Belt, which extends westwards from Belfast Lough to Donegal Bay and Clew Bay. The passage of glacial ice in the Ice Age caused the land to corrugate, building up little hills of clay, sand and gravel. The many islands in Clew Bay are the tops of drowned drumlins.

Two miles from Sligo, via the Maugheraboy road, is the famous megalithic cemetery of Carrowmore, the last resting place of the vanquished Firbolgs. The scattered cemetery extends over several townlands and is some one-and-a-half miles by half-a-mile in area. It contains dolmens, stone circles and cairns with underlying sepulchral chambers. It is the largest group of megalithic remains in these islands.

Unfortunately, this monument stands in typical drumlin countryside. Once the landowners discovered the underlying wealth of sand and gravel, their ignorant exploitation caused the most appalling devastation. According to George Petrie, the distinguished antiquarian of the last century, there were at one time over 200 sepulchres at Carrowmore. By 1900 they had dwindled to eighty-five. 'This remarkable series of ancient monuments', says Petrie, 'excepting the monuments of Carnac in Brittany, is, even in the present state of ruin, the largest assemblage of the kind hitherto discovered in the world.'

Destruction continued in the twentieth century. In 1926 a local farmer, digging in a sandpit, unearthed twenty-four skeletons. By 1937 the number of monuments had been reduced to sixty. At the last count there were no more than twenty-five. To add insult to injury, as recently as 1983 the Carrowmore

The prehistoric cemetery at Carrowmore, drawn here in 1879 by W.F. Wakeman, is said to be the burial place of the Firbolgs vanquished at the Battle of Moytirra. It contains chamber tombs and other monuments now unfortunately greatly diminished in number.

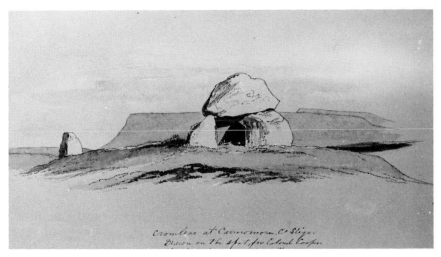

Another Wakeman drawing of Carrowmore, showing a cromlech, with Ben Bulben Mountain in the background.

Another cromlech at Carrowmore. It has never been discovered how these massive stones were placed in position.

locality was designated as a refuse dump by Sligo County Council. As with the scandal of Wood Quay in Dublin, it took outsiders to help to point up the horror of this desecration. Dr Goran Burenhult of the University of Stockholm, who had excavated at Carrowmore from 1977 to 1982, found the position 'completely intolerable from antiquarian, tourist, environmental, scientific and moral points of view.' A group of eighty-two foreign students at the International Yeats Summer School also protested. Five local residents took the matter to the High Court seeking a permanent injunction against the Council. Having failed, they lodged an appeal to the Supreme Court based on the Council's contravention of the National Monuments Act 1930. After a six-year legal battle, judgement was given denying the Council the right to dump at Carrowmore. In a historic ruling, Judge J. McCarthy said: 'The Council was wrong; it reckoned without that combination of private advantage and public spiritedness that sometimes goes to law to bring bureaucracy to heel. It reckoned without the present plaintiffs.' Meantime, part of the twenty-five acre site was acquired by the Board of Works who have plans to open it to the public, using an existing farmhouse on the site as an information centre. Without doubt, it will be an attraction as irresistible as Stonehenge.

MAEVE'S TOMB AND THE TÁIN

At Carrowmore we're in the shadow of Knocknarea. At its summit, 1,078 feet high, stands Miscaun Maeve, a man-made, prehistoric stony mound exposed in the starkness of its isolation to the four winds of heaven for some two thousand years. It is reputedly the tomb of Queen Maeve of Connaught who, with her husband, King Ailill, lived in the first century of the Christian era. An envious, jealous and selfish Amazon, Maeve was, by all accounts, prepared to sacrifice whole armies of men to satisfy her merest whim. She was probably the most powerful Irish woman of all time, even attaining the status of a Celtic goddess.

The awe-inspiring dimensions of her tomb perhaps reflect the dread loyalty she commanded, even in death. It is estimated to contain 40,000 tons of stones, is 200 feet in diameter and 630 feet in circumference at its base. The slope to the crown is 80 feet and the diameter of its flat top is 100 feet. It is greater by far in its immensity than it appears from the lowlands. 'Myths suffuse the air like spray,' said Seán O Faoláin. 'One look at that flat-topped plateau of Knocknarea, one hint of its associations is enough to subdue all disbelief.'

Thankfully, unlike some megalithic monuments in Ireland, stones are not usually taken from Miscaun Maeve by souvenir hunters. In fact, the opposite is the case, for there is a custom discouraging such vandalism. On your first visit to the tomb you get a lucky wish if you bring a stone up with you and add it to Maeve's mound. Not long ago an unfortunate American visitor got her instructions mixed up. Instead of bringing a stone up, she brought one down from the tomb and took it home, all the way to the United States. She must have met somebody who knew better, and warned her of the possible consequences. Conscience-stricken, she posted the stone back to Sligo, c/o the postmaster. With it she enclosed three dollars to get a 'gosoon' - it would, of course, be a 'gosoor' in Sligo - to take it back to its rightful place on Miscaun Maeve!

From Ransboro crossroads on its eastern side, facing Sligo city, Knocknarea is an easy climb. The weather must be clear though, or you'll be wasting your time. The west face of the mountain is sheer cliff, best viewed from Culleenamore on the Ballisodare-Strandhill road. A wide-angle view can be had from Dromard on the opposite side of Ballisodare Bay where, like all the mountains surrounding Sligo city, the scree-strewn cliffs in the distance give an impression of extensive waterfalls.

Queen Maeve's name is best known for her part in the story of the Táin Bó Cuailgne. Following an argument with her husband as to which owned the greater treasure, she ordered their respective possessions to be brought before them. Herds of cattle and hordes of horses were assembled. There was nothing

19

to choose between the wealth of the husband and that of the wife. To settle the matter once and for all, their jewels, their crowns and their gorgeous regalia were brought out. Still there was no difference to be discerned. But then King Ailill was found to own a magnificent white bull which couldn't be matched by his consort.

Promptly, Maeve despatched royal missions through the country in search of a bull of equal excellence. One emissary returned informing Maeve that the King of Ulster had a great brown bull without equal in the land, and he would be honoured to present it to her. Delighted, she prepared to take possession and so restore equal standing with her husband. But shortly afterwards another messenger turned up with startling news: the King of Ulster had made no such promise, and if Maeve coveted his bull so greatly then she must come and get it, which meant a fight to the finish. Incensed at such insulting behaviour, she ordered the Connaught army to invade Ulster. Despite the heroic defence mounted by the fabulous Cúchulainn, a raiding party got hold of the Ulster king's brown bull of Cooley, and brought it back in triumph to Maeve.

Ailill's resident white bull took an instant dislike to the new arrival from Cooley. A fight followed, the stamping of hooves and the clash of horns being heard across the land. Having won the fight, Maeve's new brown bull bore away on his horns the vanquished white bull of Ailill, tossing him in the air and shaking him to pieces as he went. Gaelic mythology leaves us to guess at the degree of domestic bliss in the royal house of Connaught in the wake of this epic struggle.

As is the case with all stories in Celtic mythology, there are variations of the Táin Bó Cuailgne. The oldest version is contained in the twelfth century Lebor na hUidhre, the earliest surviving manuscript in Irish. Repaired and rebound in recent years, this national treasure is in the safe-keeping of the Royal Irish Academy.

Like most serious visitors to Sligo, the writer and traveller William Bulfin climbed Knocknarea. 'There is an epic suggestiveness which you cannot miss,' he said. 'You cannot keep your hold on the present while you are up there.' Which reminds me of an experience I had in 1950 when I believed my hold on the present was reasonably firm. Accompanied by a highly excited fox-terrier, I had climbed the mountain on a cloudless summer's day. Sitting in the heather at the summit, the view took in all 360 degrees of the compass, from Nephin and Croagh Patrick in Mayo, to Slieve League in Donegal, from Ben Bulben to the Ox Mountains, with the Curlews in the far distance beyond. At my side the dog sat contentedly, his forepaws side-by-side, stretched on the ground, as he too seemed to relish the peace, the sun's warmth and the superb view.

I saw no movement until a hare suddenly appeared in front of us. No more

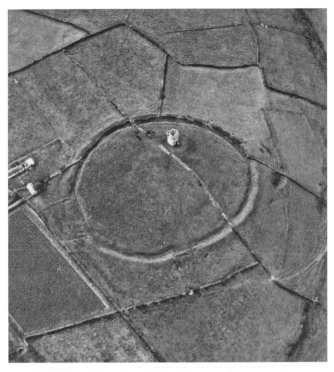

Carrowmably rath and Martello tower, Dromore West.

than a few yards away, it sat up on its haunches, staring at us for the better part of a minute. My first thought was to keep still, for fear that the dog would be alerted, would give chase and get lost on the mountain. As if satisfied with its scrutiny, the hare loped off at no great speed, while the dog, though now fully alert, made no attempt to follow. Very disturbed, he simply looked at me with a cringing air of dreadful fright. Suddenly I felt cold. I had often heard of apparitions of Queen Maeve on the mountain: a tall strong woman in her thirties, dressed in white with a sword hanging at her side. Fair enough! Most probably that would have been at night. But in the mythology of Sligo evil spirits were said often to take the shape of hares, and hares moved in broad daylight. Add to that the belief that horses and dogs have an instinct for the presence of an evil spirit. I am not superstitious, and perhaps it was merely an instance of Bulfin's 'epic suggestiveness', but I have never forgotten that hot-cold, high-noon experience in the summer sunshine on the lonesome summit of Knocknarea.

Chapter 2

The Coming of Christianity

THE BARONIES OF SLIGO

Preceding silage and the combined harvester, hay was 'made' in the summer as forage for the winter. Here is a horse-drawn rake gathering the hay before building it into cocks. In the background is King's Mountain, part of the Ben Bulben range.

Irretrievably interwoven, superstition and mysticism were once the breath of inner life in County Sligo, as they were throughout Ireland. Nor did the coming of St Patrick do much to change things, at least not immediately. A wise missioner, Patrick tolerated much that was pagan, allowing it to live alongside his teaching until Christianity might take a firmer hold. It is inevitable, therefore, that as we proceed on our tour of the region, several influences will frequently reappear: stories of the long-ago, mixed in with very odd ideas and pagan practices, some still to be observed in country places, particularly around the numberless holy wells with which County Sligo is blessed.

Excluding his passage through the county as a youthful escaping prisoner, St Patrick made two visits to Sligo as a missioner, spending in all some seven years there, a considerable period in a mission to Ireland which lasted for twenty-nine years in total. While he enjoyed the place - the fish was good, and he was partial to fish - he also found a sly strain of resistance in the conservative Sligo pagans. Indeed, there were parts of the county he found to be no-go areas. His travels are recorded in terms of the county's six baronies: Carbury, Coolavin, Corran, Leyney, Tirerill and Tireragh, subdivisions of the county once administered by a baron. They will figure again as we continue our tour, so it is well to note their positions.

Tirerill covers the south-easterly region, including the villages of Ballisodare, Collooney, Riverstown and Ballinafad. It stretches from the southern shore of Lough Gill in the north to Lough Arrow at the foot of the Curlew Mountains in the south. It was once the territory of Ailill, husband of Queen Maeve, and his posterity was there in the time of St Patrick. The barony covers nearly 76,000 acres.

Corran lies in the south-midlands of the county and is bounded by Mayo and Roscommon. It includes Ballymote town, the village of Buninadden and the Hill of Keash. It derives its name from Corran, a Tuatha de Danaan harper who was granted the territory in recognition of his musical talent. South Sligo is known internationally for its association with Irish traditional music. Corran extends over 45,000 acres.

Coolavin is south of Corran, close to Boyle. Covering 25,000 acres, it is the smallest of the six baronies because its remaining half lies outside the boundary of County Sligo. It includes Lough Gara where lake dwellings, or *crannógs* were recently discovered.

Leyney is bounded on the south-west by County Mayo, on the north by the Ox Mountains, and on the east by the baronies of Corran and Tirerill. With over 121,000 acres, it is the biggest barony. Leyney was 'behind the mountains', a place of mystery to me as a child. If I caused annoyance I was told the mountainy men of Leyney would come and carry me off through the Ladies' Brae, a wild pass in the Ox Mountains. Once somebody showed me a postcard - an exotic sunny scene, probably in some south sea island - and told me it was Leyney. Somebody else told me there was a railway there, and at that age I had railways on the brain. This information didn't fit in with mountainy men. But there must have been a grain of truth about the ferocity of these people, because Leyney was St Patrick's no-go area.

Tireragh, with 90,000 acres, stretches eastwards from the river Moy in County Mayo to Ballisodare Bay. The Ox Mountains bisect County Sligo from west to east, and Tireragh lies between this rugged range and the Atlantic. The road linking Sligo and Ballina traverses the barony of Tireragh from end to end, and in its course provides an infinite variety of scenery. Skreen, where we lived, is right in the middle of the barony. 'Up Tireragh!' was a sort of

23

whoop or war-cry one often heard, without quite knowing why Tireragh should be either up or down.

Carbury covers the north-east region, including Sligo city. On the west it is bounded by the sea, and on the east by County Leitrim. While Yeats knew the whole of County Sligo intimately, the barony of Carbury is 'the deep heart's core' of the Yeats Country, an area extending some dozen miles in all directions from Sligo city. The name of Carbury is taken from Cairbre, the third of the eight sons of Niall of the Nine Hostages, a pagan high king who ruled from Tara around the end of the fourth century.

Niall was a man of astute political ideas and had colonial ambitions. To keep the country effectively under his control he took as hostage the eldest son of each of the five regional kings of Ireland. Provided their royal sires behaved themselves, the sons would be allowed to live in a manner befitting their princely rank. But in the event of a rebellion by any of those lesser kings, Niall promised the respective father his son's head upon a dish. The arrangement worked so well that it allowed Niall to turn elsewhere for mischief, even to indulge ideas of overseas colonisation. In various sorties into Wales he took four more hostages, the sons of local Welsh chieftains. Hence his name: Niall of the Nine Hostages.

ST PATRICK

Amongst the prisoners brought from Wales in A.D.402 was a sixteen-year-old youth, Patricius, the son of a noble Roman called Calpurnius. The boy was sold as a slave to an Ulster chieftain called Miliuc, and for six years he herded sheep on the slopes of Slemish Mountain in County Antrim. Skerry Church in Magheramully is believed to be the site of Miliuc's house where the boy lived. A hollow in a nearby stone is called 'St Patrick's footmark'. From it, legend says, ascended the angel, Victor, after appearing in a vision to the friendless youth.

Eventually, Patricius escaped. Reaching Sligo (other areas make the same claim), he was taken aboard a ship bound for Gaul. It was while studying the Christian faith at Auxerre that the young man had his dream: a call to return to Ireland, bringing the new Christianity with him. In A.D. 432, directed by Pope Celestine, and now an ordained bishop, Patrick landed in Ireland with the none-too-easy mission of making Christians of the inhabitants.

Having crossed the Shannon into Connaught, Patrick first entered County Sligo as a missioner near Geevagh in the modern barony of Tirerill. From the bleak heights of the Moytirra plateau, where the pagan Firbolgs and the Tuatha de Danaan had had their set-to, he could view Ben Bulben and Knocknarea through the Collooney Gap in the Ox Mountains. There are at least four holy wells in the Geevagh locality bearing his name. A lichen-covered gable of a small ancient church on a low eminence near Ballinafad village, on the Sligo-Boyle road, marks the site of the first church - a wooden one, of course - founded by St Patrick in County Sligo.

Lingering in the vicinity of Lough Gara, he founded a church at Kilnamanagh. Near the ruins is a St Patrick's well. From the modern barony of Coolavin he crossed into Mayo. His forty days and forty nights of prayer and fasting on the peak of the 2,510 foot Croagh Patrick, Ireland's holy mountain, are recalled by an annual pilgrimage on the last Sunday of July. Here he prayed for the success of his Irish mission, and it was here too that he banished the demons and the snakes into a little lake called Lough na Corra at the southern base of the mountain.

Killala in County Mayo takes its name from a church founded there by St Patrick, and then assigned to St Muredach, the patron saint of the locality. In the twelfth century Killala became the see of the diocese to which it has given its name. St Patrick's Cathedral occupies the site of a medieval church. The eighty-foot round tower is a remnant of an early monastery.

From the shore opposite Killala, St Patrick returned to Sligo over the river Moy. It wasn't easy. The bar of the river has always been a treacherous crossing place. There are wrecks strewn about to prove it. First there were floods. Then, having reached Bartragh Island in mid-stream, Patrick was stoned by a mob. His reaction wasn't exactly saintly. To those living at the mouth of the Moy, and to their posterity, he promised endless ill-luck. Retaliation followed on the Sligo side of the river. Three poison-giving wizards overtook him as his train re-assembled, but they failed to injure him as he was well-guarded. We tend to picture St Patrick as a lone and bearded aesthete, slogging along the rain-soaked pathways through the endless forests of Ireland, blessing wells and kindling dampish Paschal fires to bring the light to a pack of pagan savages. Whatever about the savages, Patrick was no lonesome wanderer.

Never depending upon the natives, he travelled with a troupe of faithful vassals. His company was self-supporting. They had their own milking cows, steers and goats, with herdsmen to look after them. Patrick's personal staff included a cook, a chamberlain, a charioteer, a boatman, a strong-man, a bell-ringer, even a brewer. His female staff consisted only of embroiderers for making vestments for presentation to his new foundations around the country. He employed a scribe for keeping records, and a hospitaller for the proper entertainment of guests and the distribution of alms to the poor. With this formidably sophisticated outfit it wasn't surprising that he took the natives by storm. He was half way there before he opened his mouth to say the first Pater Noster. Besides, Patrick wasn't the first Christian missionary to arrive in Ireland. Bishop Palladius has that distinction, though his mission failed.

The Patrician train paused at Carrowmably, just north of Dromore West on the Sligo-Ballina road. A commanding position 300 feet above sea-level, this was the site of a rath, the outlines of which may still be seen, despite the depredations of the British authorities in the last century in building a Martello tower at the centre of the rath. Given a clear day, the view is stunning, taking in the whole coast of County Sligo and all its mountains, bays and inlets. The eastern half of the barony of Tireragh lies at one's feet, its undulations giving the effect of a vast relief map.

In my childhood, we quite wrongly called the Carrowmably Martello tower the 'Castle of Dromore', like the song. From where we lived it stood out on that western hill like a fairy castle in a picture book. How visible it might be from day to day was one of the many ways local farmers had of forecasting the weather. Meantime, alas, it has lost its stature on the horizon, for the County Council has erected a huge water-tower nearby. Progress has dwarfed our 'Castle of Dromore'.

On his way through Tireragh, Patrick established many churches and blessed wells. Aughris, Tober Patrick, and Dromard come to mind, the last something of a mystery to a small boy. Beside a graveyard and enclosed by a surrounding wall at the foot of the Ox Mountains, the place was littered with penny pieces, threepenny bits, pieces of rag, hairpins, cheap medals and cheaper crucifixes, all green and rusting from the weather. Here was an example of plain pagan superstition and mixed-up Christian piety still rampant in the twentieth century.

Even more intriguing, an old ash tree grew close by. About fifteen feet up, its bole parted into two thick branches between which there was a hole about two feet deep. This, I was told, was another holy well which miraculously filled with water once a year, on 29 June, the feast of Saints Peter and Paul. A man balanced himself up there handing down mugs of holy water, and still the level didn't drop - so I was told! Once, on my own, I climbed up and peeped inside the 'well'. Sure enough there was water, but it was raining like hell at the time - and it wasn't 29 June. The first dents in my faith were inflicted at a tender age.

St Patrick kept to the north side of the Ox Mountains because the people of the baronies of Corran and Leyney strongly rejected Christianity. Their conversion was left to St Attracta at a later date. The nearest Patrick got to Leyney was Tubber Tullaghan, through a mountain gap from Lugawarry, which is on the Sligo-Ballina road about three miles west of Ballisodare. There is a signpost to Coolaney (not to be confused with nearby Collooney). Tubber Tullaghan must be visited. In addition to its being one of St Patrick's blessed wells, it is also the setting for the magic well which is the centre-piece of the Yeats play *At The Hawk's Well*. Nearby is the Hawk's Rock, a forbidding natural cenotaph rising massively from its mountain setting.

Near the summit of a lofty rock, an unlikely situation for a well, Tubber Tullaghan is accounted 'one of the wonders of Ireland'. Its water is uninviting. With alkaline constituents, it is brackish - 'the pilgrims thus combine hygiene with religion', according to the Sligo historian, W.G. Wood-Martin. Although it is on the mountain, legend says its water-level rises and falls with the tide in Ballisodare Bay. Legend also says that a taste of its water gives immortality. The Yeats play hinges on this idea - an old man's fruitless wait for fifty years to snatch a taste of the elusive water from that magic well. Its enchantment is said to include a brace of sacred trout, only ever seen by the faithful. Although they have often been caught, cooked and eaten, they are still present in the well as lively as ever. For all its legend, Tubber Tullaghan is something of an anticlimax, but is worth a visit for the wild romance of its setting.

At Killaspugbrone Point, in the drifting sand just north of Strandhill, the lonely ruins of an ancient church crown an elevated graveyard. There is an element of doubt, but it is thought possible that these are the actual ruins of the church founded there by St Patrick and assigned to the care of Bishop Bronus. It was while in this area that Patrick, while performing his ablutions, shed a tooth, which ended at the bottom of a stream. When night came the tooth 'cast up a splendour like one of heaven's bright stars'. It was retrieved and preserved in a twelve-inch-square reliquary known as the Fiacal Pádraig (Patrick's Tooth). By the seventeenth century it was the most venerated relic in Connaught. It is now in the National Museum in Dublin.

While still in County Sligo, Patrick was involved in an angry incident with some churlish fishermen on the Duff river who refused his request for fish. On the spot he roundly cursed the Duff river. A little further on, nearer the present Bundoran, he blessed the Drowes river because little boys fishing there gave him some of their takings. We're told that 'even little boys take fish there still ', and a Drowes salmon is the finest in Ireland.

Near the Duff river is Patrick's Tobar a'Bhearrtha (the well of the shaving) where he used to shave. Being a Roman citizen - and of aristocratic nobility at that - Patrick was clean-shaven, like Julius Caesar, or Pontius Pilate, or any other self-respecting Roman. Statues and paintings of the clean-shaven Patrick were destroyed at the time of the Reformation. In the eighteenth century they were replaced by the mass-produced Italian monstrosities that wrongfully gave him a beard. So it was a clean-shaven St Patrick who finally crossed the Duff and the Drowes rivers, passing from County Sligo into Ulster, where no more than the rest of Ireland, the success of his mission is still somewhat in doubt.

ST COLMCILLE

St Patrick's lapses from sainthood were venial beside those of St Colmcille, a vengeful, vindictive man, who, for his misdeeds, paid the penalty of banishment from Ireland. In the sixth century he founded a monastic settlement at Drumcliff, five miles north of Sligo. Surviving there is part of a round tower (the only one in County Sligo), the shaft of a tall plain cross, and a twelfth century, thirteen-foot-high cross with sculptured figures from the Old and New Testaments.

St Colmcille had two scores to settle with the High King, one Dermod Mac Cerbhaill. Curnin, a Connaught prince, had quarrelled at a feast at Tara. With the High King in pursuit, Curnin took refuge with Colmcille. Despite the pleadings of the saint, King Dermod murdered the prince in his presence. The second grievance arose when Colmcille, as a guest of St Finian, secretly copied a psalter lent him by his host. When Colmcille refused to give this copy to Finian, the problem went before the High King for judgement. King Dermod pronounced: 'To every cow its calf, to every book its copy.'

Refusing to accept this verdict, Colmcille sought the help of his Ulster relatives. In A.D. 561 an army of 3,000 men, headed by Colmcille, assembled at Cooldruman (Cuildrevne), on the slopes of Ben Bulben. Heading the king's army was the injured party, St Finian. Both men prayed publicly for success. Colmcille, aided by an angel, won the battle, thousands of men were slain, and the king had to award the copy of the psalter to Colmcille.

Lost temporarily in 1497, the book remained in the O'Donnell family, the Ulster chieftains, and was always carried by them as a talisman whenever they went into battle. A descendant, Sir Richard O'Donnell, eventually deposited it in the Royal Irish Academy. Amongst the vellums in the Academy, the Cathach, or the Psalter of St Colmcille, is the oldest extant Irish manuscript of the Psalter. It was said to have been written in Latin in the late sixth or early seventh century. Its decorated shrine, or container, is in the National Museum. Incidentally, a mural of the Battle of the Books at Cuildrevne, by Bernard McDonough, the Sligo artist, can be seen in the County Library in Stephen Street, Sligo.

Banished to Iona in Scotland, Colmcille's penance was to convert more people to Christ than had fallen in the battle of Cuildrevne. From Iona he spread Christianity in the north of England long before Augustine ventured into the south.

Chapter 3

The Middle Ages

Guarding a ford over the Garavogue river, Sligo's strategic position on the pass round Ben Bulben ensured it a restless military future. Christian teachings and continuous local skirmishing having weakened the moral fibre of the Irish soldiery, the Vikings saw their opportunity. In A.D. 807 a raiding party 5,000 strong landed on the north coast of County Sligo, and devastated the country-side. Monasteries, including the foundation on Inishmurray Island, were destroyed, monks were murdered, and every village, including Sligo, was burnt.

Endemic petty rivalries and jealousies amongst the Irish chieftains were fomented by the invaders who used the opportunity to over-run Connaught, and indeed, most of the country. The High King, Malachy, managed to rid Dublin of the Vikings, thereby taking 'the collar of gold which he won from the proud invader'. Malachy was in turn deposed by Brian Boru, thus ending, after nearly six centuries, the royal dynasty of Niall of the Nine Hostages.

Brian Boru went on to establish a place and date in Irish history known to every Irish schoolchild: he finally routed the Vikings at the Battle of Clontarf in 1014.

The Irish bickering resumed, culminating in the elopement of the forty-four-year-old Dervorgilla, wife of Tiernan O'Rourke of Breffni Castle, near Sligo. The 'degenerate daughter of Erin', as Thomas Moore the poet called her, is said to have had an affair with Dermot Mac Murrough, King of Leinster, after which Dermot's peers deposed him. He sought and received the help of Henry II of England, grandson of the Norman William the Conqueror. As a result the Anglo-Norman invasion of Ireland took place in 1169 and thereby hangs our woeful tale of seven hundred years of blood and sweat, of tears, toil and hunger.

Ptolemy, the second century geographer, described a city called Nagnata on the north-west coast of Connaught, said to be the site of the present city of Sligo. Local legend has another story: the original city stood on a plain now over-spread by Lough Gill, whose islands are the tips of one-time hills. The remains of buildings are said to be visible on the lake-bottom on sunny days. Wood-Martin tells of a tourist who asked a boatman had he ever seen these buildings. 'In troth I have,' he replied, 'and shure, on a still summer's day, won't you see the smoke from the chimneys rising up in the air from the lake.'

Thomas Moore immortalised the idea of the sunken city:

> On Lough Neagh's banks as the fisherman strays,
> When the clear cold eve's declining,
> He sees the round towers of other days
> In the waves beneath him shining.

One way or the other, Sligo was probably no more than a conglomeration of wooden huts set down near a river ford until the coming in 1239 of the Anglo-Norman, Maurice Fitzgerald. Having dispossessed O'Donnell, the Tirconnell chieftain, of his Connaught holdings, and recognising the importance of Sligo for strategic purposes, Fitzgerald, then Lord Deputy and Chief Justice of Ireland, built the Castle of Sligo in 1245 on the elevated site of the present City Hall. Twelve years later he built Sligo Abbey, presenting it to the Dominicans, who are still in Sligo. Possession of the castle passed to and fro between the Anglo-Normans and the Irish, and later between the local militant Irish chieftains, the O'Connors and the O'Donnells. By 1516 the O'Donnells were in possession of both the castle and the town of Sligo.

To subdue the petty chieftains of Ireland, Tudor policy was to show them the folly of their ways: their lives lived in 'uncivil, rude and barbarous fashion, destitute of the true knowledge of God, and ignorant of their duty to the Imperial Crown of England.' O'Connor Sligo duly went to England, making his submission in person to Queen Elizabeth at Hampton Court. He returned with a title, Sir Donnell O'Connor, Lord of Sligo, but he was a less popular man. On his death in 1588 (he is buried in Sligo Abbey), he was succeeded by his nephew, Sir Donough O'Connor, who lost face locally by aligning himself with the English. To rectify the situation, Red Hugh O'Donnell, with 2,000 Irish troops, attacked and defeated Sir Conyers Clifford, with 2,500 English, on the slopes of the Curlew Mountains. To convince Sir Donnell O'Connor Sligo of the death of his ally, Clifford's severed head was displayed before him in Collooney Castle before its dispatch to Dublin Castle, while the body was sent for burial at the island monastery of the Holy Trinity in Lough Key.

After the submission of the Irish chieftains to the English throne about the mid 1500s, the country lay prostrate from years of strife. Nevertheless, the expropriation of land continued. The insurrection of 1641 was really an attempt by the original owners to recover lands of which they had been deprived. The chieftains of County Sligo united and laid siege to the English soldiers occupying Sligo Castle. After eight days the besieged soldiers surrendered. Mercifully, most were safely convoyed to Boyle.However, some twenty Protestants decided to remain in Sligo. For their own safety they were given accommodation in the gaol. Through error, a mob gained access, murdering all of the unfortunate refugees.

Sligo paid dearly for this wanton act. On the night of 1 July 1642, Sir Frederick Hamilton, a grantee of confiscated Irish lands, and one of the cruellest and most cold-blooded men ever placed in command of an army, advanced on Sligo to avenge the gaol massacre. His soldiers had instructions 'to destroy with fire and sword all they could come at', and they did just that. As Tadhg Kilgannon, another Sligo historian, relates: 'The work of destruction began at once, and in a very short time a circle of raging flames surrounded the town, and lines of flame ran along the various streets, the houses which for the most part were framed with timber and covered with thatch, igniting, in that dry and warm season of the year, like tinder'.

A diary kept by one of Hamilton's officers speaks for itself: 'A party sent towards Sligo where we met a number of rogues (Hamilton's name for the Irish), hurt divers, killed three, brought home their heads to our Colonel, with a lusty prisoner, who was hanged next day ... Killed about thirty in three cabins, and hanged our guide, who died a most obdurate villain ... Killed and stript many of their best men ... Sent a party of horse and foot upon the O'Connors and the O'Harts where we had good sport in killing nearly sixty of them, with all their three Captains, and Captain Teige O'Connor's wife ... Took prisoner Charles M'Guire, after breaking his leg to cure him, and had him laid on a barrow to the gallows where he rayled at us for not getting a soldier's death after serving in France and Spain ... We killed over three score of their best men, with divers other gentlemen, whom our boys stript, to God's holy name be the praise and the honour ... Burned and killed in their houses upwards of three score persons ...' And so it goes on.

HAMILTON'S HOLOCAUST

In the most dreadful night through which Sligo has ever passed, the worst excess of Hamilton's holocaust was his destruction of the Dominican Abbey. His officer's diary records the horror as he witnessed it from his Colonel's point of view: 'When he [Hamilton] crossed the fooard, which brought him close to the Friary [the Abbey of Sligo], he fired their brave Mass house and Friary, where, it is said, we burned many good things which people had given for safety to the friars, and all their superstitious trumperies belonging to the Mass. It was thought some of the friars themselves were burned; two of them running away were killed in their habits. As we finished this work, and giving God the praise for the success, our Colonel held it fit to haste homewards, notwithstanding our wearisome march and hot service that night in burning the towne of Sligo, where it is confest by themselves was destroyed that night neere 300 souls by fire, sword, and drowning, to God's everlasting great honour and glory, and our own comfort.' Satiated, Hamilton, with his brutal army, returned to his castle in Manorhamilton in County Leitrim.

But that wasn't the end of Sir Frederick Hamilton. Having left the town a vast charnel house, he has had, ever since, to contend with the powers of Sligo legend and literature. In *The Curse of the Fires and of the Shadows*, Yeats has left, in less than 2,000 words, a filmic vision of Hamilton's firing of the Abbey of the White Friars of Sligo. In its directness and simplicity, it is as moving a piece of descriptive prose as any to be found in English literature.

It was a summer night when Hamilton's Puritan troopers attacked the Dominican Abbey. 'As the door fell with a crash they saw a little knot of friars gathered about the altar, their white habits glimmering in the steady light of the holy candles. All the monks were kneeling except the abbot, who stood upon the altar steps with a great brass crucifix in his hand. "Shoot them!" cried Sir Frederick Hamilton, but nobody stirred, for all were new converts, and feared the candles and the crucifix.' Presently Hamilton's bodyguard of five obeyed and began to shoot. 'The noise and the smoke drove away the mystery of the pale altar lights, and the other troopers took courage and began to strike. In a moment the friars lay about the altar steps, their white habits stained with blood.'

With straw lit from a holy candle the Abbey was then set ablaze. 'The red tongues of fire rushed up towards the roof, and crept along the floor, setting in a blaze the seats and benches and making the shadows of the troopers dance among the corbels and the memorial tablets.' When the troopers emerged from the blazing Abbey, 'before them were blazing houses - behind them shone the Abbey windows filled with saints and martyrs, awakened, as from a sacred trance, into an angry and animated life.'

Yeats goes further. He includes the legend of Lugnagall (the steep place of the strangers), the mountain that rears itself over the southern shore of Glencar Lake. On leaving Sligo, Hamilton's bodyguard - the five murderers - became detached from the main company, and lost their way in the darkened woods. Hearing music, they followed it to where they found an old man sitting by a fire of sticks, his old white horse tied to a tree. Ordering him to mount, and to guide them to the right path, the six set off. The old man kept quickening the pace until the six were thundering forward. Suddenly a yawning chasm opened before them, the lake below throwing up shafts of rippling moonlight. Their impetus carried five men and five horses over the cliff to their deaths below. A ghostly guide had made some amends for the massacre of the White Fathers, and for the destruction of the Abbey of Sligo.

Shortly after Hamilton, the little town was to endure attack by another monstrous man. A ferocious and bloodthirsty bigot, Sir Charles Coote would spare nobody, not even infants. 'Rarely,' we are told, by Tadhg Kilgannon, the Sligo historian, 'did either commander or soldiers show any compassion; and

Four miles north of Ballinafad on the right hand side of the road to Sligo, and two miles from Heapstown cairn, is Castlebaldwin, an L-shaped seventeenth-century fortified house. Nearby is the village of Castlebaldwin.

when one soldier did, and protested against the murder of infants, a fellow-soldier told him that it was safer have them killed; that nits would become lice.' With 4,000 foot and 500 horse Coote laid seige to Teige O'Connor and his small force. As usual, Sligo was the target because of its strategic position. Promised 'fair and honourable quarters', O'Connor capitulated. Promises meant little to Coote. O'Connor's men were promptly 'disarmed, stript, and foully murdered, so as never a man escaped'.

CROMWELL AND THE JACOBITES

In 1645 Malachy O'Queely, the Archbishop of Tuam, marched on Sligo with 2,000 men in an attempt to dislodge Coote and the Parliamentarians. The Archbishop failed. He was slain at Cleveragh - a beauty-spot overlooking the Garavogue river - being 'first shot with a pistol ball and next mangled and despatched with swords.' Without a ransom of £30, Coote refused to part with the Archbishop's body to return it for burial in Tuam. The hated Parliamentarians retained possession of Sligo until 1649, only to be succeeded by the tyranny of Cromwell.

The Irish were treated as savage beasts, rather than as human beings. A priority of the Cromwellian forces was the destruction of all children. 'The treatment has this disadvantage,' says Froude, the English historian, 'it must be carried out to the last extremity, or it ought not to be tried at all. The dead do not come back; and if mothers and babies are slaughtered with the men, the race gives no further trouble; but the work must be done thoroughly.' Children who survived these butcheries were, when ten to fourteen years old, shipped as slaves to the West-Indian sugar plantations - which accounts for the continuing prevalence of Irish names in those parts.

The Cromwellian Settlement involved the dispossession of the Catholic Irish of their lands, and their banishment 'to hell or to Connaught'. Rather than being another plantation, the settlement was a transference of wealth and power from Catholics to Protestants. Those banished to Connaught were not allowed to occupy 'a belt of ground four miles wide, beginning at Sligo and stretching along the coast to Limerick.' This reserved portion was awarded to officers of Cromwell's disbanded army, men who could be trusted to guard the coast on behalf of England. Thus, in County Sligo alone, over 63,000 acres were handed over to Cromwellian soldiers while the old 'county families', the O'Connors, the Mac Donoughs, the O'Garas, the O'Harts and the O'Dowds, fled across the sea.

The ascent to the throne of England by a Catholic king, James II, sent spasms of apprehension through the Protestant ascendancy in Ireland. They could well lose all they had gained under the Cromwellian Settlement. The challenge of William of Orange to take the throne from James did nothing to allay their fears. Preparing for the worst, the Protestants of Sligo developed a siege mentality, worsened by a rumour that they were to be massacred by the Jacobites. Arming themselves, in 1689 they occupied the Castle of Sligo - which had been re-built by the Cromwellians. Soon they were strengthened by the arrival of a Williamite army under its commander Lloyd. Boyle, twenty-six miles away, was occupied by the Jacobites. From Sligo, Lloyd led a raid, reducing Boyle and leaving 700 dead. On the march back to Sligo he carried off 10,000 cattle.

Leading an army of Jacobites, Patrick Sarsfield a spirited commander, attacked the Williamites in Boyle, pursuing them to Sligo, where they were joined by the garrison in a headlong retreat towards Ballyshannon via the Ben Bulben route. The Jacobites held out in Sligo throughout the summer of 1690 while the Williamites were winning the battles of the Boyne, Athlone and Aughrim, ensuring the Protestant succession. The last western garrison to surrender, the Sligo Jacobites set out to help those besieged in Limerick. They arrived only to find the Treaty of Limerick had just been signed on 3 October 1691, ending the Jacobite War.

Chapter 4

Downs and Ups

In managing Ireland in the eighteenth century, England substituted the law for the sword. The Popery Code - the Penal Laws - were introduced to keep Irish Catholics in a state of permanent subjection. All priests had to be registered. They were also obliged to take an oath renouncing the elements of Catholic teaching, which, of course, they refused to do. Consequently priest-hunting became an industry: £50 reward for a bishop, £20 for a priest, and - as Catholic schools were banned - £10 for a Papist schoolmaster. Intolerable pressures and prohibitions were placed on Catholic landowners, the whole exercise being geared towards the eradication of Irish Catholicism. In these activities, County Sligo was a microcosm of the country.

For instance, the authorities in Dublin Castle sought information throughout Ireland as to the possessions of Papists, particularly horses over the value of £5. In 1715 the Provost of Sligo was most obligingly detailed in his reply to the request of their Excellencies, the Lords Justice in Dublin: 'I did immediately go with the High Sheriff, Pierce Gethin, Esq., and George Ormsby, Esq., to search all suspected places within the borough, and found one cask of gunpowder in the hands of one Charles Fallon, a Papist, who refused to take the oath of abjuration as did three others of the best sort of Papists of this town, for which I sent them to His Majesty's Gaol, as I did also another Papist, who harboured two non-juring priests, and had one of them in bed in his own house when we went to search. I have ordered a good guard of thirty staunch Protestants to duty in this borough ... I thought it my indispensable duty to let you know what is done in this borough in order to their Excellencies command.'

To their everlasting credit, not all the Protestants of County Sligo availed of the opportunities open to them to do down their Catholic neighbours under the Popery Code. In fact, the property of many Catholic families was saved by legally transferring it to Protestant neighbours, to be restored in more favourable times. One exception has found its way into Sligo legend and literature. For safety Charles O'Hart of Cloonamahon, near Collooney, transferred his land to his friendly Protestant neighbour, Laurence Bettridge. But when the time for restitution came, Bettridge adhered to his legal hold on the O'Hart property - perhaps because by then the inheritor was a priest. In 'The Ballad of Father O'Hart' Yeats records the immorality of the transaction:

> Good Father John O'Hart
> In penal days rode out
> To a shoneen who had free lands
> And his own snipe and trout.
>
> In trust took he John's lands;
> Sleiveens were all his race;
> And he gave them as dowers to his daughters,
> And they married beyond their place ...

Cloonamahon belonged to the MacDonaghs until the break-up of Celtic rule in the sixteenth century. The lands later passed to the O'Harts, who, as we've seen, were deprived of them. Because of this affair, Bettridge had to leave County Sligo, after which the lands passed to the Meredith family. Owen Tweedy (1888-1960) in his book, *Gathering Moss*, writes charmingly of childhood holidays at the Elizabethan mansion of Cloonamahon, the home of his mother, Alice Maud Meredith (1855-1896). Situated on a high hill opposite the Gothic gateway to Markree Castle, the home of the Cooper family, about two miles out from Collooney on the road to Boyle, Cloonamahon became the County Sligo Sanatorium. The name of the place was enough to strike terror into the hearts and minds of a generation who stood in mortal dread of tuberculosis. Handsomely rebuilt, it later became the novitiate of the Passionist Fathers. Now under the North Western Health Board, it is a home for mental defectives. Incidentally, the deprived Father John O'Hart eventually became the Bishop of Achonry where he served from 1735 to 1739.

In the eighteenth century, Ireland suffered under trade restrictions imposed in favour of British producers. In the 1770s England was at war, not only with America, but also with France, Holland and Spain. She was obliged to withdraw every available British soldier from Ireland. Stripped of troops, the country was open to invasion. To protect their interests, Irish Protestants took to arms. Led by the Earl of Charlemont, a Protestant volunteer movement sprang up. Country gentlemen in splendid uniforms flaunted themselves patriotically as captains and colonels. Parades were held and resolutions were adopted pledging support for free trade and the defence of Ireland. But things became more serious. The volunteers paraded in Dublin with a cannon bearing a placard: 'Free Trade Or This!'

Meetings were held and resolutions of support adopted throughout County Sligo. The 'Loyal Sligo Volunteers' paraded regularly, inspired by martial music. Trade restrictions on Irish products generated an anti-British feeling amongst Protestants. The 'Tirerill True Blues' in Sligo made the position clear with their declaration: 'That we will oppose the execution of all such statutes as the usurped authority of a British Parliament has hitherto enacted, or may hereafter attempt to impose on a country whose great wish is to be free.' As always, the loyalty of Loyalism is easily dented when material considerations are at stake.

The Irish Volunteer Movement reached its political peak in 1782 when 100,000 men in arms assembled in Dublin's College Green, while within the Parliament House, Henry Grattan proclaimed the independence of the Irish Parliament. The country rejoiced, and for eighteen years Grattan's Parliament presided over an independent kingdom sharing a monarch with Britain.

The exploitation of the masses continued, but this was Ireland's greatest period of imaginative industry: the Bank of Ireland was founded; the Custom House and the Four Courts were built. Rutland Square (now Parnell Square) was completed and Merrion Square begun. Fate struck her next paralysing blow with the Insurrection of 1798.

THE BATTLE OF CARRICKNAGAT

Agitation for Catholic emancipation and reform of the self-seeking minority Dublin government increased. Since the successes of the American and French revolutions, republican ideas were percolating into Ireland. Attracted by the ideas of liberty, equality and fraternity, Theobald Wolfe Tone, a young Protestant lawyer, founded the United Irishmen, and sought the help of France. The French fancied the idea of having a go at England via the back door, so to speak. Their first expedition reached Bantry Bay in December 1796, with Tone now an officer serving in the army of France. Appalling weather conditions, however, prevented a landing.

Dublin preparations for a rebellion were fumbled, resulting in a courageously desperate but uncoordinated effort at insurrection. Through the summer of 1798 there were sporadic outbreaks by ill-equipped peasants, hundreds of whom lost their lives. The blind bravery of the boys of Wexford has such a special place in Irish song and story that the peasant efforts elsewhere tend to be overshadowed. There was, for instance, in August 1798, the Battle of Carricknagat, near Collooney, in County Sligo. Carricknagat was a brief, hotly-fought confrontation with the British, ending in victory for the Franco-Irish forces. That sounds grandiloquent, but is true enough as far as it goes. Frankly, there was something unreal and pretentious about every aspect of this French-backed expedition, except that large numbers of innocent Irish peasants suffered needlessly and dreadfully in death and destruction.

To understand what led up to Carricknagat, and to its consequences, we must briefly go outside County Sligo to Killala in Mayo, or, perhaps more

correctly, to La Rochelle, north of Bordeaux, on the west coast of France. From there on 5 August 1798, Major-General Humbert sailed in command of three French frigates: the *Concorde*, the *Franchise* and the *Médée*. With over 1,000 men, 3,000 rifles, 400 pistols, and an additional 1,000 French uniforms, in which to dress Irish peasant volunteers, the French were well aware of their inadequacy in trying to invade a country already laced from end to end with British barracks and blockhouses. At best, their trip would be a diversionary tactic to embarrass the common enemy. And the Irish - always in prayerful expectation of some foreign armada bringing deliverance from their conquerors - the Irish would, of course, rally round in ignorant enthusiasm. William Rooney, the poet and Arthur Griffith's boyhood friend, has caught that sense of expectation in 'The Men of the West':

> The hill tops with glory were glowing,
> 'Twas the eve of a bright harvest day
> When the ships we'd been wearily waiting
> Sailed into Killala's broad bay;
> And over the hills went the slogan
> To waken in every breast
> The fire that has never been quenched, boys,
> Among the true hearts of the West.

On 22 August the French expedition arrived in Killala Bay, landing at Kilcummin, five miles north of Killala. Once unloaded, the three frigates left immediately for France. Humbert had as good as burnt his boats. Rumour preceded him. By the time he reached Ballina the local yeomanry had fled - not before creating a reign of terror amongst the population. It was a pleasant surprise, therefore, when after nightfall an affable army, colourfully accoutred, arrived by the old road, called Bothar-na-Sop, dishing out uniforms to likely lads. The people came out, and in gratitude lit the way for these harbingers of freedom for Ireland. Ever since, 1798 has been known locally as 'the year of the French'.

From Ballina Humbert turned west, and via Crossmolina passed through the picturesque country between Mount Nephin and Lough Conn. At Lahardaun he bivouacked, where, we're told, his men were fed by the locals. Contradictory records tell us the locals fled into hiding in the caves and crevices of Nephin. At any rate, from behind a stook of flax in a high field one little boy stood his ground. He watched the blue-coated infantry, their bayonets catching the sun, as battalion after battalion disappeared between the high cliffs, through the Windy Gap heading for Castlebar. The little boy never forgot. In time he became the distinguished Archbishop of Tuam, John

MacHale (1791-1881), whose statue by John Henry Foley stands near the cathedral.

What happened in Castlebar is the best-known incident of the Humbert expedition. The English, under General Lake, got out fast, 1,800 Highlanders and local yeomanry making the thirty-mile dash to Tuam with only brief stops to fire farm houses and to loot. Irish history knows this escapade as 'The Castlebar Races'. The French camped on The Lawn in Castlebar, beside the residence of George Bingham, Earl of Lucan, the hated tyrant who, like his Cromwellian brethren, had fled in face of danger. Castlebar raised two Irishmen to places in history. Jubilant in triumph, Humbert made John Moore President of Connaught, under the French. The son of George Moore of Moore Hall, County Mayo - and a forebear of George Moore, the novelist - John Moore died in Waterford Prison and is buried on The Lawn in Castlebar. An attempt on Humbert's life was foiled by his Irish aide-de-camp, Bartholomew Teeling, a young Ulsterman in the service of the French Army. Of Teeling more anon.

Though rumour had it that the English were massing at Tuam, Humbert decided to march on Sligo, that is, in the opposite direction! His advance-guard reached Collooney at 11 a.m. on 5 September 1798, halting a few hundred yards further on, while the mile-long main body caught up.

A meal was being prepared when a farmer from the hills gave the alarm. From the heights he'd seen English troops coming from Sligo. Hardly had he delivered his warning when the sound of a cannon confirmed the Franco-Irish forces were under attack. Colonel Vereker of the Sligo garrison had decided that attack was the best method of defence. With 600 men he had advanced to Carricknagat just north of Collooney. The terrain is a pass in the Ox Mountains through which, today, run the Dublin to Sligo road and railway. On the east is the Ballisodare river and the hill called Union Wood. On the west are the rocks and outcrops of the foothills of the mountains. With superior local knowledge, Vereker used an eminence called Parker's Hill to hide one of his two field guns, manned by an English marksman named Whitters.

Humbert sent one column back to Knockbeg to cross the river there, and advance through a valley behind the high ground, the object being to attack Vereker from his rear. His second column advanced slowly parallel with the river, suffering grievously in the process from Gunner Whitters on Parker's Hill. An hour of intense fighting passed, and still the French were unable to silence Whitter's gun. Then something astonishing happened - a display of heroism in the mould of Jack-the-Giant-killer. Spontaneously, a horseman galloped forward from the French ranks, rode swiftly up Parker's Hill, his pistol drawn, and at the closest range shot Whitters dead. That officer was Bartholomew Teeling. His gallantry, and Humbert's superior skill and strategy ensured victory for the Franco-Irish. Both English cannon were captured, Vereker and his force fleeing back to Sligo, leaving some sixty dead and one hundred English prisoners taken.

Had Humbert realised it, Sligo was there for the taking. Vereker created terror amongst the town's population, principally Protestant, as he evacuated and fled northwards to Ballyshannon. The townspeople followed, leaving the streets of Sligo as silent as the night. Referring to the matter, the next issue of the *Sligo Journal* reported: 'During the above anxious period no business of any kind was done, and nothing was seen in our streets save a few, a very few, citizens, who with a holy fear kept a desultory watch. We printed not, for what had we to say? or to whom publish our tale of woe?'

Believing he was dealing with the main English force under General Lake, Humbert, the unpredictable, marched away, this time in an easterly direction. Reaching Dromahair in County Leitrim, he decided that the captured artillery and cannon were only an encumbrance. So they were thrown into the shallow river Bonet, where the enemy eventually recovered them intact.

Once more Humbert turned. His men dragging their own heavy guns, he trailed through Manorhamilton, and then southwards through Dromkeeran, followed by an unfortunate peasant rabble, unknowingly tramping to their doom. English forces, now under Lord Cornwallis, continually harassed Humbert's rearguard, while they also revenged themselves by devastating the countryside through which they passed. These non-stop running skirmishes caused Humbert finally to halt at Ballinamuck in County Longford. Here he ceremoniously laid down his arms. Having fulfilled the formalities of surrender, the French became particularly cossetted prisoners of war. Not so the unfortunate peasant insurgents who had supported Humbert for three weeks. Their choice was death on the battlefield or the hangman's rope. At the end, 500 of them, most in French uniform, lay dead at Ballinamuck. One thousand escaped, but for weeks afterwards, corpses were found throughout the surrounding countryside.

Notably, there were no French fatalities. Instead, they were lavishly entertained like heroes, as they were ferried to Dublin by canal in easy stages. Everywhere they were cheered on by the music of English army bands, while Dubliners crowded to Dawson Street to see their arrival at the Andrew Falkiner Mail Coach Hotel, which stood on the site now occupied by the New Ireland Assurance Company. Next day, escorted by a military band, they embarked at the Pigeon House on a specially-prepared transport for Liverpool and France. Forgotten was the tragedy they had left behind amongst the innocents of Mayo, Sligo, Leitrim and Longford. In their mopping-up operations the hangmen were busy for weeks.

As for Captain Bartholomew Teeling, the twenty-four-year-old hero of

*Captain Bartholomew Teeling, an Irishman serving in
the French army, was the hero of the Battle of
Carrignagat in 1789. This monument, overlooking
the battlefield, was erected in 1898. The photograph
precedes the loss of Teeling's right hand thanks
to the marksmanship of a passing Black and Tan!*

Carricknagat, and Humbert's aide-de-camp, he was refused prisoner-of-war treatment. Instead, he was singled out as a traitor, and, like a common criminal, was publicly hanged outside Arbour Hill Prison - still wearing his French uniform, with the addition of a tricoloured cockade in his hat. Thus died one of the most romantic and chivalrous characters of the '98 Rising.

Ireland isn't noted for the beauty of the monuments it raises to its patriot dead. Sligo, however, showed discretion and taste in its memorial to Teeling. A life-size figure stands on a tall granite plinth surmounting a rocky height from which Teeling looks for ever over the battlefield of Carricknagat. The memorial was erected in 1898 to mark the centenary. As a child I remember the bitter indignation aroused locally when a passing Black-and-Tan took a pot-shot and blew away the upraised right hand. Teeling is also remembered in Sligo city where there is a street called after him.

The Humbert Summer School was launched in 1987. Amongst many functions, the 1798 memorial, unveiled in 1898 by Maud Gonne MacBride at the Pearse Street-Humbert Street junction in Ballina, was re-dedicated by her son, Sean MacBride, at its new site at Bothar-na-Sop. The principal ambition of the school appears to be tourist-promotion, and of course, 'to forge closer links between France and Ireland.' It could well be that the enigmatic General Humbert may do more for the Irish people in the twentieth century than he could ever have hoped to achieve in the eighteenth.

Chapter 5

'Sligo Is No More'

POVERTY AND POTEEN

The Act of Union in 1800 was Britain's retaliation for longterm Irish insubordination, and particularly for the effrontery offered by the insurrection of 1798. If, as a result, Dublin lost its glitter and became a provincial city, the Irish countryside became a greater-than-ever rural slum. Far and wide poverty prevailed. In County Sligo thousands were living at the barest survival level. The future held no prospect of improvement. Indeed, conditions must worsen, for while the density of the population increased, the size of land-holdings diminished as fathers subdivided their plots to accommodate their adult sons. The process continued until land holdings were often no more than mere potato patches.

To pay the rent to the landlord and the tithe to the parson, farmers turned to any source that might provide money. A cow on a rope was grazed on 'the long acre' - the roadside. Men went to England and Scotland as seasonal farm labourers. Those with more initiative turned to the secret distillation of poteen. Some burned kelp, the seaweed containing carbonate of soda and iodine, used for manufacturing soap and glass. If all else failed husbands and wives were forced to beg. Humiliated, they never begged in their own locality. With a spade he went in one direction, with a bag she in another. An ailing man, no longer able to work, would pass on his miserable holding to his children, and then take to the road as a beggar - a sort of social suicide. Life in rural Ireland had been reduced to a state of hopelessness.

In the early 1800s County Sligo harboured two groups of young men, each intent on its own very different ambition. The Sligo Bucks were akin to their Dublin namesakes, hell-raising sons of the wealthy, or as Terence O'Rorke, the Sligo historian puts it, 'the degenerate descendants of Cromwell's officers and soldiers.' They indulged in duelling, in drunken orgies, and they delighted in terrifying the Papists with their warped sense of amusement. A typical story tells how one night they forced a passer-by into a coffin, nailed it down and placed it on the parapet of a bridge so that the slightest movement inside would topple it into the river below. Nor were these Bucks confined to the town. They had several hell-fire clubs throughout the county.

The second group had a more serious intent. They were the Threshers, one of the many secret societies of the time, and their aim was to fight the unjust system under which Catholics had to pay tithes to Protestant clergymen. A Reverend Leslie Battersby, Rector of Skreen, went further and demanded 'family money', a tithe based on the number in the family. Sir Jonah Barrington challenged him. The case was tried in Sligo before a judge and jury who threw out Battersby's claim.

Because of poverty and the barter system, tithes were paid in sheaves of corn, sold later by the parson to the highest bidder. Being non-sectarian, the Threshers set out also to curtail the exorbitant charges made by priests. They got their name from their habit of stealthy night-time visits to those who ventured to buy the tithes from the parson. They punished these miscreants by threshing the sheaves and carrying away the corn. In her quaint fashion, local historian Lady Morgan saw the nub of the problem. She wrote in her *Patriotic Sketches*:

> I am at present residing in that part of Ireland where the association of *thrashers* first arose. I am consequently surrounded by those who formed that association; a peasantry poor, laborious, vehement and enterprising; capable of good or ill, in the extreme of both; left to the devious impulse of either; but oftener impelled by the hardest necessity to the latter, than allured to the former, by kindness, precept, or reward. Punished with rigorous severity when acting wrong, but neglected, unnoticed, and unrecompensed when acting right; forming the last link in the chain of human society, and treated with contempt because unable to resist oppression.

The activities of the Threshers became so serious that an investigative commission had to be set up in Sligo. As a result two Threshers were sentenced to public flogging, six to transportation, and one to be hanged. That was the end of the Sligo Threshers.

CHOLERA

A potato famine occurred in 1817, and another in 1822. These famines were always followed by epidemics of famine fever. Worse occurred in 1832 when an epidemic of cholera hit Ireland. It took some months to reach Sligo, one of the last places to be affected. The result was an overwhelming calamity, with up to one hundred deaths a day. It would take over another fifty years before Robert Koch (1843-1910), the German bacteriologist would identify the causative bacillus, called the comma bacillus because of its shape. Yet the Sligo doctors of 1832 knew of the contagiousness of this acute disease, and how it was so easily spread. Knowing it was in the country, they took what they hoped might be preventive measures to save the town of Sligo.

Suspicious that cholera had an atmospheric origin, they sent up kites. They analysed water and advised boiling. They burnt tar-barrels in the streets. They

44

'Boycotting' means a conspiracy of coercion to prevent all dealings - social, commercial or otherwise - with a person. The name derives from its first use in 1879 against Captain Charles Boycott, agent for Lord Erne's estates at Lough Mask House, County Mayo. 'Boycott' became a dreaded word in the stormy days of the Land League.

advocated the liberal use of whitewash inside and outside the house. But cholera still hit Sligo, and when it did, the more ignorant citizens threatened vengeance on the doctors, for they believed it was their interference that had brought this disaster on the town.

Cholera caused more suffering in Sligo than in any other place in Ireland. At the height of the epidemic people were falling dead in the streets. Carpenters couldn't cope with coffin-making. Corpses were tied up in sheets smeared with pitch and rolled into mass graves. Whole families were wiped out, and undertakers with their 'cholera carts' knocked on doors to collect the latest dead. In their great haste to dispose of infected corpses, some people were buried alive. This gave rise to terrifying stories.

In their fear of death, citizens took to the country roads in a stampede out of Sligo, but the farmers resented them as the harbingers of disease. They built walls across the roads to stop migration in any direction. They ceased to bring their products into the town, after which food went short. A great silence fell as the population was decimated, the streets becoming as green with grass as the fields. A newspaper heading read: 'Sligo is no more.'

The aftermath of the cholera visitation lasted for years. All five of Sligo's doctors had died, along with those who came to assist, a total of eleven doctors. Passing a friend's house, a Doctor Coyne saw the cholera cart outside. He enquired and was told his friend was dead. Nonetheless, he went in and examined the so-called corpse, only to find the victim wasn't dead. He resuscitated him, and a few days later the patient was better, but the doctor was dead. There was also wholesale death amongst nurses, but not a single priest died!

Indirectly, Bram Stoker owed his love of the macabre to the Sligo cholera epidemic. His mother, Charlotte Thornley, was a young woman living in Sligo at the time. Her stories about coffin-makers knocking on people's doors, and grave-diggers burying people alive, fired the youthful imagination of her once sickly son who spent so much of his childhood at home with her.

THE GREAT FAMINE

The Great Famine was another source of horror stories, for nowhere were there more dreadful results than in Sligo. The famine is written about today as if it had occurred without warning, like an earthquake or a hurricane. The symptoms had existed for decades: an ever-increasing population (up to 8.3 million in 1845), eking out an existence on ever-diminishing holdings of land, and entire dependence upon the potato for subsistence.

As early as 1834 Sir Robert Gore-Booth, grandfather of the patriot Countess Markievicz, foresaw social disaster. He bought 800 acres of land at Ballygilgan near his home at Lissadell, by offering the tenants land elsewhere, or their passage to America. According to prevailing circumstances, he was not obliged to show such feeling. As a landlord, he could have evicted them without further ado. Most chose to emigrate, and a ship was chartered. Legend claims it was unseaworthy. At any rate it sank when hardly outside Sligo Bay with the loss of all on board. Though all this happened years before the Great Famine, local tradition chose to retail it as Sir Robert's coffin ship loaded with famine victims. This wasn't quite correct.

In 1844 the eight-year-old newspaper, *The Sligo Champion* (still going strong), in its leading articles tried to call attention to 'the looming disaster in the West'. While these articles were quoted in foreign newspapers, nothing was done by way of precaution. In 1845 the Mayor of Sligo pleaded on behalf of the unemployed and hungry citizens. 'The disposition of the poor is different to that in other parts of the country,' he said, 'they are not prone to drinking.'

Much nearer to the brink of disaster, a strange manifestation was seen near Collooney. O'Rorke, the Sligo historian, records it graphically: 'On 3 August 1846 Mr Cooper of Markree Castle observed a most singular cloud, which extended itself over the last of the range called the Ox Mountains in the County of Sligo, accurately imitating in shape a higher range of mountains somewhat more distant; afterwards an extremely white vapour, resembling a snowstorm, appeared along the southern declivity of the range. Mr Cooper remarked to a friend that he thought this vapour might be charged with the fluid causing the disease in the potato ... That same night the blight fell upon the whole of that side of the mountain where they had witnessed the strange appearance.'

The difference between the famine and the cholera epidemic, fourteen years earlier, was that this time town and country were equally affected, at least at the outset. As conditions worsened, many country people went into Sligo clamouring for admission to one or other of the poorhouses, hoping for food of any kind. To qualify for such relief under the Poor Law, those who held more than a quarter of an acre had to give up their land. This, and fear of fever and dysentery then rife in the poorhouses, meant that many others, now *in extremis*, starved to death amidst fields of fat cattle and grain grown specifically for export to pay the rent. Local merchants understood the export business, but not how to import. Hence such stupidities as a relief ship lying in the bay, too overladen with American grain to cross the bar into Sligo.

Incidentally, William Pollexfen, a wealthy Sligo shipowner, and grandfather of W.B. Yeats, had a consignment of corn on its way by sea from Broadhaven to Sligo for transhipment to Liverpool when it became becalmed off the Sligo coast. Starving locals rowed out, terrifying Pollexfen's crew. They filled their boats with life-saving corn, but not before some were caught. These were tried and sentenced to terms in Sligo gaol.

One of the byproducts of the famine was what was known in Sligo as 'souperism'. Certain Protestant organisations fed the starving, provided they converted to that faith. As a boy I heard references to families which, though I didn't understand the nuances, I suspected weren't complimentary: 'That fellow came of poor stock, didn't his family take the Protestant soup.'

The most active proselytising centre was the Protestant colony at Doogort in Achill. The Reverend Edward Nangle was its missionary-in-chief. The avowed purpose was the conversion of 'Romanists'. The children of 'Romish families' were taken in, housed, fed and educated. However, Mr and Mrs S.C. Hall, an English couple who toured Ireland and published *Ireland: Its Scenery, Character, etc.* in 1843, were critical of the Reverend Nangle's idea of Christianity. On the road they met a thirteen year old boy in tattered clothes. His name was Hart and he came from Sligo. He had been given three shillings and then thrown out by Nangle because he was a bad boy. He was told to go back to Sligo, a journey of some sixty miles. On their side-car, the Halls took him back to Nangle, who confirmed the boy's story. They pleaded for him, as a repentant prodigal. Nangle refused, 'giving no account whatever of misconduct that shut him out from mercy. We therefore took the lad upon our car out of Achill Island, and adding a few shillings to his scanty store, sent him to beg his way to Sligo.'

The year 1847 was the high-point of famine death. Graveyards were enlarged, becoming so overcrowded that they built up into hills. The sliding coffin was introduced: loaded, it was held over an open pit and the bottom slid out like a drawer, dumping the contents into the so-called grave. Thousands upon thousands of bodies passed through the same sliding coffin. But the demand for even this degree of decency eventually became too great. Mourners resorted to bundling their dead into creels made of salley-rods, and slung over a donkey's back. An aunt of mine heard all this verbatim from her old aunt who, as a girl, had seen the bundled-up bodies in donkey creels going for burial in Kilglass, County Sligo.

The holding of inquests became a charade, lasting until the system broke down. A note to a local coroner reveals the hopelessness of the situation:

Riverstown,
Co. Sligo.
8th February 1847

Sir,
 Half-a-dozen starvation deaths have been reported to Mr. Grant this evening, and he directs me to write to you to request you will attend here early tomorrow to hold inquests.

James Hay, Head Constable.
Alexander Burrows, Esq.

But Mr Burrows was unequal to the work he had to do. In one day, although he tired three horses, he succeeded in holding only five inquests. Poor progress, in as much as there were forty corpses in the district of Maugherow still awaiting his attention.

In these days of Third World famines, we tend to criticise local administrations for their ineptitude. The fumbling stupidities which attended the Great Famine in Ireland were of such magnitude as to lead one inescapably to the conclusion that it was all intentional - a heaven-sent opportunity to rid the world of the troublesome Irish. If so, the effort was in great part successful. A dying Daniel O'Connell made his last tragic appeal in the House of Commons:

Knocknashee, near Lavagh, 'The Fairy Hill', from the air.

'Ireland is in your hands, in your power. If you do not save her, she cannot save herself ... one-fourth of her people will perish unless you come to her relief.' But his plea fell on deaf ears, and in three months O'Connell himself was dead.

When all was over, Sligo was a withered and devastated countryside, and Ireland had lost two million of her people.

Chapter 6

The Fenians and the Landlords

The second half of the nineteenth century saw two movements associated with Sligo, both invoking the Pope. The first was 'The Pope's Brass Band' of 1854, the second the Pope's Sligo Brigade of 1860.

In 1852 John Sadleir, a notorious crook, teamed up with William Keogh, a self-seeking lawyer, in an unscrupulous campaign to win themselves seats at Westminster by buying votes, Keogh representing Athlone, and Sadleir Carlow. No longer acceptable in Carlow at the subsequent election, Sadleir sought to represent Sligo. Hiding his hypocrisy under a cloak of zealous Catholicism, Sadleir was supported in Sligo by the local bishop and many of the priests. Because of their parade of religion, Keogh and Sadleir, and their followers, were known as 'The Pope's Brass Band.'

Sadleir won his seat for Sligo, becoming Lord of the Treasury, while Keogh was elevated to the Bench. Sadleir swindled the public out of £1 million, and thousands lost their savings in the collapse of his complex banking empire. All of which reflects poorly on the Sligo electorate of the time, which was, in fact, as warped as its new MP.

When John Sadleir's candidacy was rejected in Carlow, and he was then accepted in Sligo, he knew he was on to a good thing. Dubbed 'a sink of political corruption' and 'the most rotten borough in the Kingdom,' Sligo at the time was just the place to attract a man of Sadleir's mentality. The electorate numbered about 500, amongst whom bribery, corruption, intimidation and the employment of rent-a-mob tactics were openly practised. A man could be paid handsomely to vote and just as handsomely not to vote.

When the strife eventually involved the wrecking of homes of electors, and the burning of their business premises, when even the clergy were being accused of exerting 'undue influence', a Royal Commission was set up in 1869 to enquire into these corrupt electoral practices. Its findings bore out the accusations. As a result, a Disenfranchisement Bill was introduced, and one year later Sligo Borough ceased to exist.

The Pope's Sligo Brigade began when Giuseppe Garibaldi (1807-1882), the Italian patriot, liberator and guerrilla-leader, fought for the unification of the various Italian states. He believed that Rome would have to be wrested from the Pope before the true unity of Italy could be gained, so he marched on the Papal States. The plight of Pope Pius IX incited the men of Sligo to form a Pope's Brigade, as had been done in other parts of Ireland. Amidst wild enthusiasm, over 150 young men embarked at Sligo port in June 1860.

Italy was disillusioning for some of these volunteers. Others grew homesick, and disgraced themselves by coming home too soon. But some suffered and died. The venture somehow missed being the 'holy work which would render their names memorable not only in the history of their own county, but also in Europe'. Their greatest reward may well have been when all Sligo went wild with excitement as it welcomed home the surviving heroes of the Pope's Brigade.

THE *ERIN'S HOPE*

The ineptitude of the organisers of the abortive Fenian Rising of 1867 was never so obvious as in the mishandling of the American brigantine, the *Erin's Hope*, when it arrived in Sligo Bay. The story has all the ingredients for a film of epic proportions: courage, weeks of nail-biting tension, pursuit by enemy warships, the effects of the raging gales of the North Atlantic on a two-hundred-ton vessel. Let's hope nobody thinks of making a film, because God help us, the local Fenians would show up so very, very badly.

On the conclusion of the American Civil War in 1865, 200,000 trained Irish-American soldiers were demobilised, all of them only too ready to fight again anywhere, as long as it was against England. To help the rising planned in Dublin by James Stephens, the US Fenians selected key personnel to man an arms ship destined for Ireland. Captain John Powell, Chief of Naval Affairs, wrote to Captain John Kavanagh:

New York City
April 12th 1867

Sir,
You will proceed with the vessel under your command to Sligo Bay on the coast of Ireland, or to any other part of the same coast of Ireland where you may more safely land your cargo and passengers. You will use every precaution to ensure the delivery of the cargo and passengers to the persons authorised to receive them.
If possible, after you land your cargo and passengers, you will return with your vessel to New York and turn her over to the proper authorities; but in case you see no chance of escaping with her, destroy her if practicable. You will in all cases use your own judgement.

God bless and speed you.
Yours fraternally,
John Powell.
Chief of Naval Affairs, F.B.
To Commander John F. Kavanagh.

For the benefit of the US Customs, the brig was allegedly carrying pianos, sewing machines and casks of wine, all neatly crated and consigned to a fictitious firm in Cuba. In fact she was carrying five thousand stand of arms, three batteries of artillery, one thousand sabres, five million rounds of small ammunition, among other things. More was intended to follow, because the poor misguided US Fenians believed that Stephens and his men in Ireland really meant to rid the country of the English once and for all.

The forty Civil War veterans who made the crossing were commanded by General J.E. Kerrigan. The name of the vessel was *The Jacknell*. On Easter Sunday in mid-Atlantic by general agreement she was re-named *Erin's Hope*. To celebrate they fired a salute, hauled down the US flag and replaced it with the Sunburst, 'Erin's war standard.' The chief engineer, Colonel Tresilian, had already mined the vessel in case of confrontation with the British Navy.

Despite a ten-day storm, they reached Sligo Bay on 10 May. All aboard signed a letter of congratulation to Captain Kavanagh for getting them safely to their destination. Displaying signals day and night brought no response from the land. Nor was there any sign of fighting. Some fishermen came alongside, but knew nothing of a Fenian rising. Captain Kavanagh and the men of the *Erin's Hope* gradually realised the information given them in New York had been grossly exaggerated.

After two weeks' waste of time it was agreed they would run the vessel into Sligo port, seize the town, and land their arms. They would dig in and wait for the general insurrection that must follow the news that an Irish-American force had landed, and that the Irish flag already floated over Sligo town. The rally would be like that shown to Humbert in 1798.

Erin's Hope was moving cautiously into Sligo when a cutter arrived with a Fenian messenger from Dublin. They were too late, the insurrection was over, he told them, as he handed over a written order:

May 25th 1867
Captain Kavanagh,
Commanding Expeditionary Vessel.

Sir,
You will proceed to the point of communication which is Toe Head, off Skibbereen, South coast of Ireland. The brig is to sail when in those waters with her jib down, but not furled on the boom. You will be met by a craft from the shore, which will approach you with jib also down and unfurled.

Unsigned, the order purported to come from the chief organiser of the Irish Republican Brotherhood. Thus ended Captain Kavanagh's plan to seize Sligo.

Leaving the bay as the dawn broke, the *Erin's Hope* was chased and narrowly missed being caught by an English gun-boat.

Although the story now moves away from Sligo, it is worth following these courageous men in their little brig as they run before the might of the British Navy for a lost cause.

Repeatedly sailing up and down the twelve-mile stretch of coast between Toe Head and Galley Head off Skibbereen, County Cork, as instructed, there was still no sign from the land. Captain Kavanagh increased his sweep to thirty miles between the Old Head of Kinsale and Baltimore - but still nothing was seen. Food and water were running low, so the expedition attempted a landing between Glandore and Galley Head. Observed, and pursued by a coastguard, they got away, only to be chased by an English gunboat. Once more they escaped, this time into the darkness.

Somewhere off the Saltee Islands on 1 June a fishing smack appeared out of the mist. It was agreed that 32 of the US Fenians would go ashore after nightfall to reconnoitre. They would re-join the *Erin's Hope* off Mine Head one week later, on 6 June. Meantime, believing he would be less obvious on the English side of the Channel, Captain Kavanagh cruised between Lundy Island and Land's End. Without knowing the fate of his friends, he was back, lying off Mine Head as arranged, one week later.

Caught landing on Ring Strand, the US Fenians had been arrested and imprisoned in Kilmainham Gaol. Indicted for treason-felony, they all got long prison sentences. Even Colonel Warren, a naturalised American citizen, got fifteen years penal servitude. As happened so often in Irish history, they had been betrayed by an informer from amongst their own company.

Having endured another week of tension, this time off Mine Head, those US Fenians still on board instructed Captain Kavanagh that it was past time to return to New York. Off Cape Clear on 12 June the prow of the brig was turned from Ireland. After one hundred days and nine thousand miles of voyaging, she landed in New York on 1 August, 1867, her cargo still intact. In chasing her in Irish waters, three British ships were lost: the *Lapwing*, a first-class gunboat lost in Killala Bay; the *Revenue*, a similar boat wrecked on Daunt's Rock, while a second-class gunboat sank in a gale off Cape Clear. So perhaps the cruise of the *Erin's Hope* wasn't entirely in vain.

THE LAND LEAGUE

Professor T. W. Moody has called Michael Davitt's Land League 'the greatest revolution in the history of modern Ireland'. Sligo was the birthplace of the League. It proved to be the movement that finally convinced British statesmen that the Irish landlord system was no longer defensible. Thus landlordism was finally abolished, making Ireland a land of peasant owners, but not before Davitt had been sorely tried, not least in County Sligo.

Famine returned in the winter of 1879/80, along with the worst weather for thirty years. A harsh winter made no difference to the evictions. The twelve-year-old Constance Gore-Booth saw the misery all around her from her privileged position at Lissadell, and she never forgot what she saw. Meantime, in a fighting speech at Irishtown in Mayo in April 1879, Davitt inaugurated a land reform movement to change the economic pattern of farming and so abolish recurring famine.

After that launch at Irishtown, the first meeting of the Land League took place at Dromore West in County Sligo in September 1879. The second, and more famous meeting, was at Gurteen in south Sligo on 2 November. An attendance of eight thousand waved green flags and heard no less than five bands. Abetted by John Boyce Killeen, a Belfast Presbyterian barrister, and James Daly, a Castlebar newspaper proprietor, Davitt proclaimed the time was ripe to rid Ireland of landlordism and rack-renting. All three speakers were promptly arrested for sedition and were lodged in Sligo's Cranmore Prison.

'The Sligo State Trials' that followed became world news, providing more publicity for the Land League than money could buy. The source of this unusual interest was a Belfast Presbyterian solicitor called John Rea, a man as odd as he was brilliant, who was retained to defend Killeen. Rea called himself 'Her Orthodox Presbyterian Brittanic Majesty's Orange-Fenian Attorney-General for Ulster.' His object in Sligo was to ridicule the whole proceedings, thus exposing Dublin Castle and its laws to public contempt.

The Resident Magistrate had risen from the ranks of the Royal Irish Constabulary. From the moment Rea addressed him as 'Mr Promoted Police-man', to the point where the Magistrate mispronounced a word and Rea rushed in to know if it was permissible for an official of the Crown to murder the Queen's English, the press reporters' telegrams poured out of Sligo. 'The situation was superb,' Davitt said, 'and some cells in Sligo Jail echoed each night with chuckling and contented inmates.' The defendants' concern was how best to prolong the priceless entertainment - the 'judicial vaudeville,' as it was called.

The star performer, John Rea, kept the show going for a week. He had 'turned the trial into a farce, and made it an international laughing stock.' The collapse of the Sligo State Trials had a profound effect, ensuring the future success of Davitt's Land League.

From time to time Sligo has produced both notable, and colourful, politi-cians. Only one has been commemorated monumentally. Patrick Aloysius McHugh, or 'P.A.' as he was known, drew Davitt's unstinted admiration. He called him 'one of the most deservedly popular members of Parliament with the very highest qualities of public and political life.' McHugh, a one-time teacher of English and science, acquired *The Sligo Champion* in 1885, when the fortunes of that newspaper were in a dismal state. Using his journalistic and editorial skills to further nationalism, he transformed *The Champion* into a markedly influential provincial newspaper. With his platform thus established, he stepped into active political life. Elected a member of Sligo corporation, he immediately became Mayor. For his so-called intimidatory articles he got a six-month sentence in Derry jail, the first of many such solitary sojourns. It says something for the quality of the man that he was elected Mayor of Sligo for five successive years.

In 1891, after the Parnellite split, the Chief, Parnell himself, appeared in Sligo for the last time. He had come in support of his candidate Valentine Dillon, a solicitor, in a highly contentious election. Reviled, as elsewhere, he was received with ugly mob-hostility. Shortly afterwards he was dead. A year later McHugh was elected as an anti-Parnellite MP for North Leitrim, his native county. For years he struggled to compose the Parnellite differences, and thus present a united Irish Party at Westminster. The result was the emergence of the Irish Parliamentary Party in 1900 under the leadership of John Redmond.

When McHugh became bankrupt in 1902, and his newspaper closed down, he simply coined a new name, *The Sligo Nationalist*, and continued his publication. A grudging local loyalist allowed that at least McHugh 'had been one of the most brilliant of the Irish members in the House, and after an "Irish scene" he had been forcibly carried out spreadeagle fashion by some of the Sergeant-at-Arms' minions. This mode of progress in England added considerably to his fame in Ireland.'

McHugh died at the age of fifty-one in 1909. His unique political contribution inspired his admirers to erect a statue of him. Local factions disputed about the site, the most prominent in the city centre. A green lamppost was removed by one faction and a foundation stone laid in its place. A rival group removed the stone and replaced the lamppost. Eventually, tempers cooled and a statue of 'P.A.' appeared at the top of a three-pillared marble pedestal, with three semi-circular ledges at its base, meant for what ... flowers perhaps. It was unveiled in 1916 by the then Mayor, John Jinks, in the presence of John Redmond.

As I remember it, the McHugh memorial, standing opposite Sligo's GPO, provided a convenient round-the-clock resting place for idle layabouts. Their years of sitting on the ledges of the pedestal had left the stone as shiny as a French-polished table-top. Meantime, progress has meant the replacement of 'P.A.' by an island with traffic lights. Now he keeps his vigil, more appropriately for such a habitual Mayor, round the corner at the front of Sligo's City Hall.

John Jinks, the unveiler of the McHugh memorial, himself created a brief

The Sligo State Trials - outside the courthouse.
The Land League, founded by Michael Davitt in 1879, became known
internationally as a result of this farcical legal episode.

sensation in 1927. As the National League's TD for Sligo-Leitrim, he disappeared from Leinster House when the Cumann na nGaedheal Government of
W.T. Cosgrave was facing a vote of no confidence. His opponents were certain
of Cosgrave's defeat. However, Mr Jinks, having heard the debate, decided to
abstain and disappeared. Thus, by the Sligo-Leitrim member's abstention, the
government was saved to fight another day.

It was thought that Deputy Jinks had been kidnapped, his disappearance
being the hottest news until he calmly turned up next day, wondering what all
the fuss was about. Seán Lemass declared that henceforward the Cosgrave
government held office only 'by the good will of a gentleman from Sligo whose
name is - or who did not answer to his name of - John Jinks' but the grass-roots
never forgot. At the next general election, the most famous TD of the time was
defeated.

Chapter 7

The Twentieth Century

ARMAGEDDON

Even in the first decade of the new century Britain and Germany were already squaring up for the greatest war the world had known. My father had left London to begin medical practice in his native Sligo. When he found a house in a reasonably central locality in the dispensary district of Skreen, then my mother and I followed. We were hardly settled in when the Great War began in 1914. Being on the reserve, my father found a locum, and re-joined the Royal Army Medical Corps. This meant trips to England for my mother and myself for as long as he was stationed there. At a camp in the grounds of Taverham Hall near Norwich, I was photographed on a charger - the soldiers' name for a horse. More frightening is a memory of waking up chilled and miserable, and being carried by a sailor down a gangway. Below I could see lights reflecting coldly in the sea as it slopped menacingly deep down between the ship and the pier. I don't know whether we were coming or going. But I do know that depression always gripped my mother on her arrival home. Understandably, I suppose: a woman with a husband, three brothers and a brother-in-law 'at the war', herself a stranger in a strange land, and the charms of County Sligo hadn't yet had time to enchant her.

The effects of emigration were everywhere. Nor was it finished. On train journeys between Sligo and Dublin I saw distressful partings: howling mothers clinging to their embarrassed teenagers until the last heart-rending moment when the train moved slowly away, and they were at last en route for Queenstown (now Cobh) and the White Star liner, bound for Staten Island, Queens or the Bronx. This meant fewer and fewer marriages in County Sligo, and fewer children for the schools. I was packed off to school at five, and my sisters started even younger, to keep up an average attendance sufficient to justify the employment of two teachers.

I loved that school - now, alas, no longer a school. There was the companionship of other children, something of which we were very much deprived. There were no children in our immediate neighbourhood, and besides, we weren't allowed to mix more than was necessary. My father was hot on signs of bad grammar, and my mother stamped heavily on even the echoes of a Sligo accent. And so, outside school, life was lonely. Miss Furey, my first teacher, read beautifully. Her stories came from books like *Told At The Feis*, tales of derring-do in mythical Ireland. There was a wood outside the window, and as she read I could see Cuchulainn and Queen Maeve and Balor of the Evil Eye, alive and well and stalking to and fro through the trees. These stories offered a stark contrast to the woods of Goldilocks, the idyllic countryside of Grey's *Elegy* and the Arthurian chivalry and romance of Tennyson which were read by the fireside at home on wild winter nights when the roaring Atlantic gales threatened to carry away the roof.

Promotion in Dunflin School meant moving to the other end of the room, to the Master's domain. Whatever else, Master Mulligan loved his Shakespeare. By sixth class we had 'done' - in considerable depth - both *Hamlet* and *Macbeth*. There was another window and another wood outside the senior end of the school, the wood covering a hillside between us and the blue heights of Knockalongy. The mathematical alignment of the trees suggested a company of infantry assailing the hill. For me, it was surely Birnam Wood come to Dunsinane.

At home the most exciting event of the day was the arrival of the postman. He it was who brought seasonal presents from English relatives and friends: Christmas, birthday, and sometimes even surprise parcels. *The Daily Mail* and *The Irish Independent* were delivered by post, a day late of course, but the news was fresh, for the period ante-dated radio and telephones. Urgent messages were sent by telegram.

The 1916 Insurrection for me made its own special impact: Mr Mortal, the postman - his real name was Morton - didn't come for a week. Rumour was added to rumour, and one sensed the grown-ups were dreadfully concerned. With a dad and four uncles in the war, I was nightly made to pray for 'the poor soldiers in France.' Now another trimming was added: 'and for the poor soldiers in Dublin.' Whether I was praying for Commandant-General Pearse and the lads or for Field-Marshal Lord French and the Tommies, God alone knew. A sense of cultural identity eluded me throughout my childhood.

Excitement ran high in Sligo whenever those imprisoned after the Insurrection were released. Constance Markievicz, Sligo's heroine, had languished as No. Q 12 in Aylesbury Prison, where, as she said, her hours slipped by 'like rosary beads of dragon's teeth.' Released in June 1917, she was invited to accept the Freedom of Sligo. She replied: 'I have no words to tell you of all I felt when I heard that my own native town of Sligo [in fact Constance was born in London] were conferring such a great honour on me. I long to see Sligo again. I used to think and dream of our hills and rivers and of the sun setting out over the sea.'

On 23 July Sligo overwhelmed Constance Markievicz with its welcome. She was the first woman - and remains the only woman ever - to receive its Freedom. In bestowing it, the Mayor said they were honouring the most

*Countess Markievicz (second from right) was the first-ever woman
to be elected an MP in Westminster, and also the first woman
to be honoured with the freedom of Sligo.*

distinguished member of the Gore-Booth family - a remark not quite accept-able to all of Sligo's upper-crust. Some thought the Countess a bit of a harridan. Even her old admirer, Willie Yeats, questioned whether she recalled

> ... the years before her mind
> Became a bitter, an abstract thing,
> Her thought some popular enmity:
> Blind and leader of the blind
> Drinking the foul ditch where they lie?

Nor did her family approve of her activities - but time was to heal all that. However, only the Sligo 'separation women' came out to make a scene. They were the wives of Irishmen serving in the British Forces. The Irish inde-pendence the Countess sought would lose them their separation allowance.

1918 brought the Armistice, and with it came the great influenza pandemic, killing more than had died in the Great War. The disease first appeared in Ireland at Maynooth College. The authorities there made a bad decision. They closed the college, sending the students home, thus disseminating 'flu' all over the country. My father was home by then. The demand for medical attention was such that he and my mother (she was a nurse) shared the work, he going east to Dromard one day and she west to Dromore, and vice versa the next day.

With the exception of war-time Christmasses in London in the 1940s, Christmas 1918, instead of being a post-war joyous one, was the most dismal of my life. We saw little of our parents, and there was no shopping spree. I never felt so cheated as when I opened my stocking on Christmas morning to find half-a-dozen lucky bags - bought hurriedly in a local shop. My only consolation was the sudden arrival of a British warship in Sligo Bay. Our windows had to be opened as she fired off salvo after salvo, sending great spouts of sea water high in the air over Aughris Head. If the Navy's intention was to intimidate, all it did for me was to exhilarate. I couldn't understand why some of the locals, whose windows were broken, cursed the British as the everlasting scourge of the world.

1916 AND THE NEW RESURGENCE

The resurgence of nationalism which followed 1916, and particularly the landslide victory of Sinn Féin in the 1918 general election, gave a much-needed boost to public morale. Resentment grew against the Royal Irish Constabulary, if only for the fact that they were Irishmen carrying arms on behalf of Britain. They came to be looked upon as traitors. With their local knowledge of people and places, they were the eyes and ears of the British intelligence service. The nature of the charges brought by them were often so petty as to rouse the hatred of the people.

Charges like 'unlawful assembly' could cover anything from a crossroads hooley to a game of handball against some convenient gable, or tossing a few heads of cabbage round the road at Halloween. 'Using seditious language' included singing ballads like 'Wrap the green flag round me, boys, To die'd be far more sweet' - a sentiment with perhaps some point at the time. A usually quiet young man in our locality got himself run in for shouting 'Up the green, phwite an' yalla,' after he'd had a few drinks. And, of course, to mouth a word of the Irish language was sedition of the deepest dye.

All this led to people refusing to recognise the courts. They would not remove their caps, they smoked during court proceedings, they even sang and shouted slogans. This behaviour brought longer prison terms, and greater local resentment of the police and of the magistrates handing down such vindictive sentences. This new defiance wasn't confined to youngsters. A staid Sligo alderman when sentenced to three months hard labour informed the magistrate: 'The day may come when I'll be trying you' - a home-truth all too unwelcome to those then at the top of the pile.

In County Sligo the fortunes of the RIC took another downward turn in 1919 when they shot Dr Michael Boyle of Gurteen while he was being driven to a political meeting. The fact that he recovered didn't militate against the adverse publicity.

Officially, my father was medical officer to the local RIC. That didn't seem to interfere with his popularity. In fact he was an out-spoken and unashamed unionist, an unusual combination, coming from a County Sligo Catholic family. When the time came, however, like many with unionist leanings, he with my mother, made clear their disgust at the behaviour of the Black and Tans.

On one occasion he had a run-in with the local RIC sergeant who was worrying my mother officiously and unnecessarily. In my father's absence, she had gone out on a side-car in the middle of the night to answer a call to a midwifery case. Nearing the lower road by the sea, a burning house came into view on the high road about two miles away. In the darkness and the distance she was convinced it was our house. Her driver, the patient's husband, refused to turn back - his wife, he argued, was in danger of death. My mother was helpless. On several levels, she spent some very anxious hours with that patient.

The beautiful house and stables of our neighbours, about half a mile away, had indeed been maliciously burnt out that night. The RIC repeatedly interviewed my mother, almost implying she knew more than she had told them. The questions hinged on why she hadn't raised the alarm by turning back, and whether she felt any concern for the family involved, much less for her own family. In fact, she couldn't have been more concerned. She was in a state of distress, but she was in the hands of her driver, and he had been adamant. It was at this stage my father reminded the sergeant of the respective roles of medical attendants and policemen. The whole trouble, it transpired, originated because the driver at first denied they had seen the fire, thus contradicting my mother's evidence. Eventually he owned up, adding manfully that his concern had been with his wife's condition rather than with somebody else's house on the high road.

Living in a country doctor's house during a guerrilla war, one became used to mysterious nightly comings and goings. Day or night, all sides were dealt with objectively. As a future doctor I learned very early about doctor/patient confidentiality and medicine knowing no boundaries of creed or colour.

In December 1919 the twenty-one-year-old Volunteer Martin Savage from Ballisodare was killed taking part in an attack on Lord French, the Lord Lieutenant, at Ashtown, County Dublin. We passed through Ballisodare on the day his funeral arrived. In an unnecessarily threatening display of power, the village swarmed with police. Although attended by thousands, that funeral took place with a decently quiet dignity. Nonetheless, the display of police supremacy reflected the acceleration towards the intensification of violence ahead. Martin Savage, a grocer's assistant, and all who shared his dreams were to be immortalised by Yeats:

> I have met them at close of day
> Coming with vivid faces
> From counter or desk among grey
> Eighteenth-century houses ...
> We know their dream; enough
> To know they dreamed and are dead.

THE BLACK AND TANS

Always venturesome, Sligo notched up another first in the new spirit of defiant resurgence. In February 1920, Alderman T.H. Fitzpatrick was elected Mayor. The first Republican to hold the office, he was also the first Mayor in Ireland to refuse the Oath of Allegiance to King George V, or to take his seat as a magistrate. In competition with the British legal system, Republican Courts were set up, and people rallied to them, believing in their justice. This growing Irish arrogance would have to be dealt with, and Lloyd George would do the dealing, in his own special way. He sent over the Black and Tans.

Its strategic position ensured the early arrival in Sligo of these oddly-dressed men, half soldier, half policeman. With khaki jackets, black trousers and glengarry caps, they were nicknamed the Black and Tans, a name in Irish lore that was to have evil connotations, as evil as those associated with Cromwell. They made Sligo a place of siege. Barbed-wire entanglements and pill-boxes appeared on all roads entering the town. Men were roughly frisked in a manner calculated to rouse their tempers, thus to make an opportunity to rough them up - or worse. Even country women coming to market their produce had to get out of their donkey-carts, while these toughs tumbled their pathetic belongings all over the road.

But it was when they drove through the country in their high-powered Crossley tenders that they spread terror far and wide. Coming from school we'd hear them in the distance, letting off pot-shots as they came. Terrified, we'd get behind a wall or hedge, until somebody warned us: that was quite the wrong thing to do. These wretches would shoot at anything that moved, so it was better to remain in the open. We got as far away as possible from the centre of the road, while remaining in view. A convoy of Crossley tenders would tear past, sending up clouds of dust, for this was before tarmacadam had reached the roads of Sligo.

Mikey McGovern, our nearest neighbour, with his father (in bowler hat). Gifted storytellers, their legend, myth and tales of the supernatural enthralled me in my childhood.

At night their appearance was even more terrifying. As they drove the twisty roads you could see their powerful lights turning this way and that in the night sky long before you heard the sound of their Crossley engines. Would they stop at our gate, or would they pass by? The tension was terrible, partly because you had heard grown-ups - and grown-ups knew everything - talk about these so-called Englishmen as if they were monsters.

One day, my two young sisters and I, were on a hill near the road when the Tans came by. Unfortunately the road was between us and our house, so we had to stay put, abiding by the usual advice - remain in the open. Two lorries suddenly stopped, while two which had gone ahead reversed. The Tans began leaping out, falling flat on their bellies on the grassy roadside bank, and taking aim. Thirty or forty shots were fired before we saw their target - Mikey, our nearest neighbour and his dog, Toss, in the middle of a field where he'd been counting sheep. He stood transfixed, his hands raised high, the dog cringing at his feet, as sheep fled in all directions.

As suddenly as they had dismounted, the Tans took off again leaving a deeply-shocked man and a couple of dead sheep. They could easily have shot him dead a dozen times - he had been an open target - but their mission was to terrorise the natives. When we got home there was pandemonium. The ceiling in the kitchen had fallen from the vibration, and all I got when I tried to tell my story was a stuff in the lug for being where we had been at the wrong time. As the eldest of a family you could never win.

Frank Carty, a legendary local hero and Sinn Féin leader, had made history as a jail-breaker. A gentle giant, with time for children, he was a frequent and welcome caller at our house. On one occasion, at dawn following one of Carty's brief midnight visits, our house was surrounded by Tans. Some peered through the windows at us, as others bashed on the doors, back and front. They dashed all over the house, turning everything upside down. Proclaiming her Englishry for all to hear, my furious mother told them they were nothing but scum and said she was ashamed of them. Their officer asked her why the hell she didn't go home before the Irish made a 'Shinner' of her. Relatively speaking, we got used to the Tans.

Chapter 8

Ireland's Nadir

ATTACK AND REPRISAL

The vicious pattern of attack and reprisal was established. One incident outdid another in devilish inhumanity until an eavesdropping child came to accept it all as part of normal life. Nevertheless, there were times when one knew that something particularly horrifying had happened. Adult conversation at home occasionally revealed more than was intended. The gaps could always be filled in by listening to unguarded gossip elsewhere.

Since the arrival of the Black and Tans, local revulsion against the RIC had increased. They guided the Tans, they identified their victims, and generally they acted as effective assistants in waging local mayhem. Sinn Féin resistance made life so dangerous for the local RIC that they had to be withdrawn to the comparative safety of Sligo town. In one night the vacated barracks in Strandhill, Rosses Point and Drumcliff were ransacked, leaving them unfit for any further use.

Burning of other barracks then began. Skreen, our nearest barracks, went up in smoke. As a reprisal the nearby creamery was burnt, leaving the farmers in the catchment area unable to dispose of their milk. We were becoming used to the stench of burnt-out premises, with oddments and personal bits and pieces thrown about, like wreckage thrown up on a beach. Sometimes I imagined our own house roofless and smouldering. Why such a thing should happen I couldn't tell, any more than I could reason why it was happening to so many people all round us.

An RIC District Inspector was shot dead in an ambush at Chaffpool. Next day the Tans attacked nearby Tubbercurry, burning shops and houses indiscriminately. The creameries at Achonry, Tubbercurry and Ballymote were destroyed. For this rampage the Tans had come from Sligo town, having first commandeered Dr P.J. Flanagan, a local practitioner, as their casualty officer. He was held in a military lorry throughout that night in the middle of the battle zone. Dr Flanagan never fully recovered from his experience. He died shortly afterwards.

As 1920 lumbered on, so, it seemed, Ireland reached the nadir of her agony. Bad as things were in County Sligo, they were as bad, and worse, elsewhere. The *Independent* brought its daily litany of shootings, mostly in Dublin it seemed. I had begun to take an interest in newspapers. The captions to photographs were about the height of my extra-curricular reading. With different people, one photograph appeared again and again. It was of a church doorway, with a Celtic cross standing before it. Always there was a coffin being carried out shoulder-high, most wrapped in the tricolour. In later years I would identify the precincts as those of the Vincentian Church in Phibsboro.

In October 1920 news came of the shooting of Professor Carolan, a Sligo man, in an ambush at his home in Drumcondra, where he had given refuge to Dan Breen and Seán Tracy, two prominent Sinn Féin activists. My father's sister was married to a doctor, and they lived next door. The doctor was forced to waste time examining the bodies of dead Tans, instead of being allowed to do what he could for his next-door-neighbour while he was still alive. The story bore out the cussedness of these evil men.

About this time we had a maid called Ellie. Like no one I have ever known, she was able to dramatise the already dramatic. I lapped up her stories: the man who refused to open up to the Tans and got shot through the door, the splintered wood piercing his heart; the woman who went into a room carrying a lighted lamp. A shot rang out from the darkness and through the window pane, killing her, the spilled paraffin then setting the house on fire; the little girl who refused the thirsty Tan a cup of water, but instead went to get him a cup of milk, and fell dead in the doorway with a mistaken bullet through her brain. No heroic little boy figured in these stories, but that didn't stop one's imagination taking fanciful flight.

When things had quietened in the evening, we'd toast our knees before the bars of the glowing kitchen range and wallow in Ellie's dramatisations - though I took them all for gospel at the time: the hunger-pangs of Terence Mac Swiney dying slowly - so slowly, over seventy-four days - in a London dungeon; the torture of Kevin Barry as the prison warders tore out his fingernails with iron pincers. Ellie told her stories with such conviction that I began to show reluctance in going upstairs in the dark for my father's slippers, or indeed for any reason. I got into a row, so I had to compromise: armed with a torch I'd close the shutters before I showed a stem of light. Years later, in London, I found no difficulty in coping with black-out curtains. In fact, to this day I automatically pull the curtains before I put on the light.

But Dublin and London were far in the future, and meantime we had our own troubles in County Sligo. In October 1920, four RIC men were shot dead in an ambush at Cliffony. Reprisals followed next morning. At least eight houses were burnt out, as well as Ballintrillick creamery, the Sinn Féin Hall at Cliffony, and the Grange Temperance Hall and Library. Shortly afterwards a party of respectable citizens, being driven by Nurse Linda Kearns, was arrested at Ballisodare. Rifles connected with the Cliffony ambush were allegedly found in her car. Our Ellie had it that the nurse had stripped the dead policemen, and it was their uniforms and weapons she had in the car.

The Tans who took Linda Kearns prisoner spent the night third-degreeing her for information about her colleagues. When bribes and threats failed they struck her in the face, breaking her teeth. At her court martial in Belfast she manfully took responsibility for the car and its contents, realising that, if convicted, her companions would get heavy sentences. In fact, they each got fifteen years, while she got ten. A woman of tremendous resourcefulness, Linda Kearns made history by escaping over the high wall of Mountjoy Prison. Poles apart politically, she and my father held a warm mutual understanding. Perhaps it arose from their professions.

On the date of Linda Kearns' arrest - 25 October 1920 - Terence Mac Swiney died. We had gone to school as usual, only to be sent home. The school had closed as a mark of respect. Everything all over Ireland had closed. Of all those who sacrificed themselves, the lingering death of Mac Swiney deeply affected the jaded emotions of the nation. On that sad day we arrived home gleefully announcing: 'No school today - Terence Mac Swiney is dead.'

A week later a stunned nation heard that Kevin Barry had been hanged. Nobody could believe it had really happened. Three weeks after that came the murderous savagery of Bloody Sunday when attack and reprisal left a trail of death through the streets of Dublin. Then the action was back on our doorstep: a local medical student was shot dead 'while trying to escape' - the usual Black and Tan cover-up. When they fired at random, they called it 'a precautionary measure.'

CONSTANCE MARKIEVICZ

Once, while shopping in Sligo, my mother was faced with a posse of Tans demanding identification. They had mistaken her for Constance Markievicz. It was an understandable mistake because, apart from her height, slim build, and accent, there was also a considerable facial resemblance. If they had but known, Sligo was the last place they would have found 'Madame' at that time. As Minister for Labour in the proclaimed Sinn Féin Government (the first-ever woman cabinet minister), she would have been busily engaged in some Dublin under-cover office - until, as she said herself, she was 'laid by the heels again.'

In fact, Constance Markievicz was in trouble quite soon, this time for a 'crime' committed eleven years earlier, to wit, her founding of the Fianna, her boy scout movement. She refused to recognise the court. Her mind was elsewhere: 'the leggings of the English army of occupation was one of the things that struck me profoundly at my courtmartial. Such a lot of time must be wasted polishing them!' On Christmas Eve 1920 she was sentenced to two years penal servitude. Never depressed, she was amused to observe that, for starting the Boy Scouts in England, Baden-Powell was made a baron.

What history calls the Anglo-Irish War dragged on into 1921. Murder and mayhem were still abroad in our locality. An old woman called Catty Antrim was battered to death in her cottage. The murderer was caught, and my father had to give evidence at the trial in Belfast (as yet there was no Border). The man was given life-imprisonment. Some months later he was seen in uniform, riding in a Crossley tender as he guided the Tans through the bye-ways of County Sligo.

A RIDE IN A CROSSLEY TENDER

In April 1921 two RIC men were taken from a train at Ballisodare Station. Next day their bullet-ridden bodies were found on the roadside. The last rural RIC barracks in use was at Dromore West. It was in a state of siege, with barbed wire entanglements and steel shutters with spy holes covering its windows. On 1 July 1921 a robbery was reported at the barracks. Seven RIC men set out on their bicycles to investigate. They had to cross open bogland. At Culleens the police patrol was ambushed by some thirty or forty men from the cover of a laneway.

School holidays had begun, so my father had taken my elder sister and me on a side-car to do a call. An open touring motor-car with two Tans tore up beside us in a cloud of dust, and the horse stood on end with fright. It was soon clear it was the doctor they wanted - and urgently. We were bundled into the tourer. I heard the words 'ambush' and 'injury', and I knew what they meant. We were dumped at Dromore West barracks while my father proceeded with the Tans.

From the summer sunshine of a July day we were taken in to the stuffy, lamp-lit kitchen of the barracks where a fire was roaring up the chimney. A well-meaning constable put us sitting on chairs before the fire as if it had been mid-winter. He told us not to move, our daddy would soon be back. Shortly he returned with two bars of Fry's chocolate. Tans were coming and going. Hearing their accents it impinged upon me for the first time that these disreputable brutes were indeed Englishmen.

The afternoon dragged interminably. Growing apprehension made me begin to enquire for my daddy. Where had he gone? Why couldn't we go home? The constable produced more chocolate, but I was past even chocolate. My daddy was dead - I was suddenly convinced - and nobody would tell me. They had taken him out on the bogs to murder him, and now we were under arrest in Dromore West RIC barracks. At last our turn had come, and calamity was at hand.

When next the constable came into the kitchen he didn't notice my tears. He took us outside. When I asked again for my daddy, all he said was 'Ye'er going home now. Tell ye'er Mammy the doctor'll be home shortly.' Then he hoisted us into the back of a Crossley tender. It had a wire cover overhead, ridged like a roof so that lobbed bombs would roll off. There was seating running lengthwise on either side, and this was occupied by a dozen or so Tans. Running the length of the centre was another seat on which men could sit back-to-back. Just then it was occupied by something covered with a rug. The rug wasn't long enough to hide a man's feet sticking out and wobbling with the vibration of the pot-holed road. It was the body of one of the policemen shot dead in the Culleens ambush.

Near our house a Tan soldier lifted us over the tail-gate of the tender. Then it roared off towards Sligo in a cloud of dust. We turned round and there was Mikey, our neighbour who'd been a target for the Tans a few months before. Amazement on his face, he said: 'Jesus, Mary and Joseph, but where did ye come out of at all?' Explanations followed, but the July sun was sinking into the Atlantic before my father turned up that evening.

The Truce was signed twelve days later, and five months after that the Treaty came into effect. A war-weary country thought the fighting was all over at last.

Chapter 9

Civil War

ARTHUR GRIFFITH IN SLIGO

The terms of the Treaty so divided the population that the vindictiveness shown by brother to brother in the Civil War exceeded the worst efforts of the Tans. It was as if Irishmen had learned from their one-time masters, and had decided to improve upon the method and manner of murder. As Yeats put it:

> We had fed the heart on fantasies,
> The heart's grown brutal from the fare;
> More substance in our enmities
> Than in our love.

Skirmishing marked the early months of 1922. That was when I first heard the name de Valera, a name that roused passionate argument. At home it was pronounced 'Deevaleera'. Outside, where I heard it more often, it sounded like 'Devil-era'. The connotations were clear: whoever he was, he was an ogre - the Devil - at the centre of this new terror. Anyway, our household was against him, which may help to explain why it took years to rid my mind of this childish notion originating in the pronunciation of a name.

On Easter Sunday, 16 April 1922, the eyes of the nation were focused on Sligo. Arthur Griffith, President of Dáil Éireann was due to speak in the City Hall on behalf of Cumann na nGaedheal candidates in a forthcoming election. Mayor Michael Nevin warned Griffith of the dangers of coming to Sligo. Republican forces under Commandant General Liam Pilkington of the 3rd Western Division had been disposed in strategic positions throughout the town. Free State troops with an armoured car then took up positions. The situation was too explosive for the President to dare to come.

But Griffith's telegraphed reply read: 'Dáil Éireann has not authorised, and will not authorise, any interference with the right of public meeting and free speech. I, as President of Dáil Éireann will go to Sligo on Sunday next.' Further Republican forces were drafted in - their proclamation, they declared, would be defended to the last man. Sligo had become a powder keg, and the public was greatly concerned: the skirmishing was over - the Civil War shooting was at hand.

Accompanied by Seán Mac Eoin, GOC, Western Command, and Lieutenant-General J.J. ('Ginger') O'Connell, himself a local man, Griffith arrived in Sligo. Unable to use the City Hall without confronting its Republican occupants, Griffith made his speech to a large crowd at the corner of Grattan and O'Connell streets, known afterwards as Griffith's Corner. Apart from a mistimed bullet from a youthful Republican, and a brief reply from the Free State forces, miraculously things passed off quietly, indeed so quietly that his local supporters entertained Griffith at a banquet.

Militant Republicans felt the Free State was born that day in Sligo. They had wanted a show-down. But for the good sense of their leader, Commandant General Pilkington, in keeping his men out of sight, thus defusing the explosive situation, there is no doubt that lives would have been lost. Indeed, the Civil War might well have begun in Sligo on that April day, instead of at the Four Courts two months later. Significantly, in more peaceful times, Liam Pilkington was to become a Redemptorist monk. Again, significantly, it was the arrest by Republicans of Lieutenant-General 'Ginger' O'Connell in Dublin's Leeson Street and his incarceration in the occupied Four Courts, which triggered the opening salvos of the Civil War.

During the summer of 1922 we went through as grim a time in County Sligo as any during the Anglo-Irish war. July saw full-scale war with the burning of Teeling Street and Wine Street Barracks, the Custom House, and the coastguard stations at Rosses Point and Raughley. Nightly, the town was attacked by Republican forces who swooped from the hills and retreated with the dawn. The town rocked when the Ulster Bank was blown up. Emboldened by their successes, the Republicans ambushed Free State troops at Rockwood on the shore of Lough Gill. There were fatalities and many casualties, but they captured an armoured car known as the Ballinalee, a vehicle that was to become a local legend. However, there was still sufficient decency to allow for a truce so that a Red Cross ambulance train could take the wounded to Dublin.

On 14 July the people of Sligo found themselves in another explosive situation. With the help of the deadly Ballinalee and her Vickers gun, the Republicans swooped, occupying various strategically-placed buildings. They sent an ultimatum to the Free State troops, then occupying the Courthouse. Unconditional surrender by 6 p.m. was demanded, or else. The officer commanding replied: 'My men will never surrender our barracks ... We hold these positions for the Irish people and for the Republic when they so will it.'

All was set for a bloody conflict until, to his eternal credit, the elderly Dr Coyne, Bishop of Elphin, intervened. Even in 1922, when religion meant more than it does today, the bishop's negotiations failed. When hope had gone of avoiding a battle, Dr Coyne placed himself between the two factions by moving into the Courthouse, and from there issuing his own ultimatum: come

71

what may, he would remain between the firing lines. Moved by the degree of his concern, the Republicans refrained from opening fire, and eventually evacuated their positions. Once again, Sligo was saved from destruction, this time by the noble deed of a noble cleric.

With her unexpected swoops, the Ballinalee continued to create alarm. Ballina was taken by the Republicans, and later Collooney. With the arrival of a Free State troop-train in Collooney, the town was evacuated, and a full-scale battle followed. Seventy prisoners were taken, and the repercussions of the casualty lists were felt at home. My father visited the incapacitated in their dug-outs in the mountains, often having to walk miles through slush and bogs. As well, the visits of mysterious young men to our house, mostly at night, had greatly increased.

One night I opened the door to half-a-dozen men with rifles, most wearing trilbys and trench-coats, the Republican uniform. As they propped their rifles against the wall behind the front door my father appeared, letting out one of his best barrack-square bellows: 'Did nobody ever teach you fellows how to stack rifles? Stack those rifles at once.' And like lambs they allowed him to show them how. My mother warned him he'd be brought home very cold some night, stretched on a shutter, but his relationship with the Republicans was more understanding than that. There was a degree of mutual respect.

On a sunny afternoon in August, my father was weeding his chrysanthemum bed when somebody came down the avenue and said: 'Did you hear, doctor, that Arthur Griffith is dead?' My father paused, leaning on his spade. 'If Arthur Griffith is dead,' he replied, 'he didn't die a natural death.' The remark reflected the confused and incredulous state of mind of the public. Ten days later there was the unbelievable news of Collins' death. Could Ireland take much more?

In September tragedy broke again in Sligo. The Free State Army could no longer tolerate the hit-and-run Republican raids made possible by the armaments of the now infamous Ballinalee. On 18 September, reinforced Free State troops, backed by armoured cars and field guns, advanced on Ballintrillick and Glencar, areas lying on either side of the Ben Bulben range. Closing in, the shells from their field guns proved effective in the mountainous terrain. The Ballinalee was recaptured, but six Republicans were killed. One victim was Brian Mac Neill, a son of Professor Eoin Mac Neill, the man who had countermanded the order for the 1916 Rising. The deaths of 'Sligo's Noble Six' marked one of the saddest occurrences of the Troubled Times in County Sligo.

DEATH AND DESTRUCTION

At the end of September my youngest sister was born. Six weeks later my father died suddenly, aged forty. With bridges blown up and trees tumbled across the roads, a life-saving cylinder of oxygen couldn't be obtained in time. In a model-T Ford car, its side curtains up to hide their rifles, his Republican patients followed his coffin - covered with his own chrysanthemums. Theirs was the only motor car in a long procession of horse-drawn vehicles.

Desolated though she was, my mother was gripped by a fear, a very real fear that the Free State troops might appear anywhere along the route, bringing the inevitable shoot-out. Nothing of the kind happened, but it still took all of that dreary November day to travel sixteen miles to the Cowell family vault at Kilglass. Every fourth or fifth vehicle carried wooden planks to throw across the gaping holes in the blown bridges, and we had hacksaws to clear a passage through trees felled across the roads. Within our family, our sense of doom and bewilderment matched the times we were living through, times that are vividly recalled by Yeats' 'Meditations in Time of Civil War':

> A barricade of stone or of wood;
> Some fourteen days of civil war;
> Last night they trundled down the road
> That dead young soldier in his blood ...

My father's successor was a young doctor back from England. Since his medical student days in Galway, the new man had been actively connected with the Movement, a generic term used to describe the national effort to attain freedom and peace for Ireland. His activities meant indefinite absences, when my mother would be pressed into service to do what she could. Once she was called out in the middle of the night. Those who had burnt out our near neighbours had come back. They had attacked the two brothers who were still living in the one room saved from the fire. They first shot dead the family's sheep-dog, but worse, they shot the eighteen-year-old youngest son. He died in my mother's arms.

Again, as if he had been there, Yeats caught the confusion and fear that beset us at that time:

> We are closed, and the key is turned
> On our uncertainty; somewhere
> A man is killed, or a house burned,
> Yet no clear fact to be discerned...

Shortly after the shooting there were whispers about the ghost of the black dog being seen at the house. Black dogs had a ghostly connotation in County Sligo. When we had to pass that way at night, we went in a state of rigid terror. Once in the moonlight I saw the black dog sitting in his accustomed place by the wrecked front door. I was petrified. Next day I passed in full daylight, and the 'ghost' was easily explained: habitually sitting against the whitewashed wall, the poor old dog had left an imprint sufficient to suggest his presence in the darkness. But the locals didn't want to hear my rational explanation. For them the place was haunted by the black dog, and that was that. Fearing they might know something I didn't know, I took to looking in the other direction when I had to pass that way at night.

I was still in love with railway trains. On our trips into and out of Sligo I used to pray that a train would pass on the high embankment and over the bridge at Ballisodare. It was therefore heartbreakingly exciting when the Sligo Republicans turned their campaign against the railways. A train from Broadstone in Dublin to Sligo was taken over by armed men between Kilfree Junction and Ballymote. Detaching the engine, they sent it, full steam ahead, in the direction of Sligo. It was derailed. A little later the Dublin-Sligo mailtrain was stopped between Ballymote and Collooney. Ordered out of the carriages, the passengers had to flee as a landmine blew the engine and tender off the rails.

In an orgy of destruction in January 1923, the railway wreckers bombed and burned Sligo railway station and all its rolling stock. Once again the town rocked to the explosions. On the same night the wreckers took seven locomotives out into the country, coupled them together and sent them under full steam down the line leading to the docks. Splintering the level-crossings, and smashing through a concrete buffer, some of the engines ended-up in the sea. Sligo was effectively isolated. Looking back, it seems incredible that, having rid themselves of the British, Irish nationals should resort to such mindless destruction of their country's assets.

Like it or not, we had to endure the privations of the time until de Valera's cease fire order came on 28 April 1923. Officially, the Civil War was over; unofficially, the shooting went on spasmodically for years. A saying crept into common use: 'The country isn't near settled yet.' To the end of the '20s that sentiment was trotted out on occasions of bank robberies, assassinations and other forms of idle devilry.

SUMMERHILL COLLEGE

In 1926 I became a boarder at Summerhill College, the one place in Sligo I ardently detested. Sixty years later my worst nightmare can still involve a 'battering' - the Summerhill word for a beating. Most of the pupils were country boys, many still wearing nineteenth-century knickerbockers. There were no cups and saucers. Tea was served in bowls and, like Oliver Twist, you didn't ask for more of anything. I had some affinity with day-boys. They were at least sufficiently civilised to trade and to read comics. But in the estimation

*The destruction of Sligo railway station and rolling stock
by the 'Irregulars', in January 1923.*

The Lake Isle of Innisfree, known to the unimaginative as Cat Island. It is said that Yeats became bored with the poem by which he will always be remembered!

of the priests - or professors as they preferred to be called - day-boys were dangerous dross - the last place to look for vocations for Maynooth.

However, it *was* at Summerhill College that I first heard the name Yeats, though they pronounced it like Keats. We had learned 'The Lake Isle' from Palgrave's *Golden Treasury*, and somebody had told us it was a good idea in essay-writing to use quotations. It showed erudition. For me it was a costly lesson. The football team had won something important. As a reward we were taken by motor-boat across Lough Gill to Dromahair - the first time I had seen such idyllic splendour. In the future, Ben Kiely would exult: 'Any view of Lough Gill has something about it of the beatific vision.'

Inevitably, the next week's essay was on our Lough Gill trip. It was an opportunity not to be missed. I interspersed my effort liberally with appropriate quotes from *'The Lake Isle'*. But I was wrong. My essay was read out for the amusement of the class. Throwing it on the desk before me, the priest-professor said: 'Don't be quoting that man anymore. Don't you know he's a Protestant?'

Years passed, and one day the mystery was solved for me. Some time before the incident, Senator W.B. Yeats had won himself notoriety amongst bigoted Catholics by criticising the powerful influence of the Catholic clergy. In his famous senate speech on divorce he even proclaimed the virtues of Irish Protestants: 'I am proud to consider myself a typical man of that minority. We are no petty people. We are one of the great stocks of Europe. We are the people of Burke; we are the people of Grattan; we are the people of Swift, the people of Emmet, the people of Parnell. We have created most of the modern literature of this country. We have created the best of its political intelligence.' And who dares to say Yeats was wrong?

In 1930 we left Sligo to live at 61, Marlborough Road, Donnybrook, a house just vacated by Jack Yeats, the painter. Every Christmas for years somebody in Spain sent him a large box of tangerines. I would have to hike it round to 18, Fitzwilliam Square, on the back of my bike. He would apologise, saying he must send his friends his new address, but he seemed in no hurry about it. On a similar errand I would meet him again the next year. Always he would wish me a happy Christmas, and I would reciprocate, neither of us recognising that, with our youth, we had both left our hearts and our happiest Christmasses behind us in Sligo.

PART 2

THE CRADLE OF GENIUS

Chapter 10

A Family Called Yeats

THE ANCESTORS

The Yeats family has a long association with County Sligo. The Butler prefix was introduced as a result of the marriage in 1773 of Benjamin Yeats (1750-1795) to Mary Butler (1751-1834). Their son, John Yeats (1774-1846) became Parson John of Drumcliff, where he served from 1811 to 1846. He was the great-grandfather of the poet. He is the relative invoked in the famous epitaph:

> Under bare Ben Bulben's head
> In Drumcliff churchyard Yeats is laid.
> An ancestor was rector there
> Long years ago...

In 1805 Parson John married Jane Taylor. They had a family of twelve, nine boys and three girls. The eldest, the first William Butler Yeats (1806-1862), followed his father into holy orders, and went to minister in County Down. The youngest, Mary (1821-1891), never married. She was known to W.B's generation as Aunt Micky. A farmer, she lived all her life in County Sligo.

In 1835 the Reverend William Butler Yeats of County Down married Jane Grace Corbet (1811-1876) of Sandymount Castle. They had a family of nine, four boys and five girls. The use of family names of in-laws was carried on in this generation: there was a Robert Corbet Yeats (1842-1857), and a William Butler Yeats, the second, (1843-1899). The name Isaac Butt Yeats (1848-1930) suggests an admiration for the founder of the Irish Home Rule Party. But it was the eldest of this family, John Butler Yeats (1839-1922), who was to distinguish himself. In the early 1850s, with his younger brothers, William Butler and Robert Corbet, John Butler Yeats, known then as Johnnie, was sent from County Down to the Atholl Academy on the Isle of Man, a boarding school that had all the monstrous maltreatment and torture then thought

Drumcliff Rectory, where Parson John Yeats, great grandfather of the poet, lived during the thirty-five years of his ministry.

suitable for shaping boys into manly men.

For the time being, we'll leave young Johnnie Yeats absorbing the humanities at the Atholl Academy while we trace the distaff side. The family of Susan Mary Pollexfen originated in Cornwall. Unashamedly, they were 'business', with little time for Yeatsian philosophising. Young William Pollexfen (1811-1892), a Devonshire-born lad, had at the age of twelve run away to sea. In his twenties he happened to sail into Sligo aboard an appropriately-named vessel, *The Dasher*. There he met a cousin named Elizabeth Middleton, whose husband, a local merchant, had died in the cholera epidemic of 1832. Elizabeth had a personable daughter, also called Elizabeth, and a business-like son called William. Pollexfen liked what he saw. There was a future in Sligo.

In 1837, at the age of twenty-six, William Pollexfen married the younger Elizabeth Middleton, then eighteen. He entered into partnership with her brother, thus founding the shipping and milling firms of Middleton and Pollexfen situated in Sligo and Ballisodare respectively. William and Elizabeth had a family of twelve, the two eldest being boys. William Pollexfen sent his sons Charles (1838-1923) and George (1839-1910) to Atholl. It was here that they met the lively young intellectual called Johnnie Yeats.

A SCHOOL FRIENDSHIP

Irish boys were in a minority at Atholl Academy. This, as well as Anglo-Irish rivalry, drew them together. Nonetheless, Johnnie Yeats found the Pollexfen brothers tough going. In their poor academic showing they always let the Irish side down, whereas Yeats was invariably top of the class. Despite their incompatibility, a friendship grew between Yeats and George, the younger Pollexfen. Years later, John Yeats would describe his school-friend as 'worse than a bore, he was an iceberg.' Yet George, whenever he chose, could hold spellbound a group of sophisticated English boys while he spun them Irish stories in his brogue and in his mannered Sligo style. John Butler Yeats summarised the young George Pollexfen: 'He talked poetry though he did not know it.'

Neither of the Pollexfen brothers accompanied Yeats when he entered Trinity College, Dublin, to study law. Instead, George was sent to Spain and Portugal aboard one of his father's trading steamers. Later, after some training in the Sligo office of Middleton and Pollexfen, he was posted as the firm's representative to Ballina, County Mayo, where he was to spend many years.

In 1862, at the age of twenty-three, John Yeats graduated from Trinity. He celebrated by going on holiday to Rosses Point where the Pollexfens had a summer house called Moyle Lodge. It faced southwards across Sligo harbour, looking towards haunted Knocknarea. The old friendship blossomed again, the dour, self-centred, yet companionable George, talking endlessly as they walked the countryside of the Rosses, drunk with the tang of the Atlantic and the scent of the wild iris.

Despite George's easy conversation, John Yeats' attention was elsewhere. The eldest Pollexfen daughter, Susan (1841-1900), dark, demure and unassuming, drew him irresistibly. She reciprocated the young man's interest. A whirlwind romance followed amidst the grandeur of Sligo and its surroundings, making the summer of 1862 a time of dream-like other-worldliness for these two young people. True to his indulgent style, before his holiday finished, John Butler Yeats had announced his engagement to Susan Mary Pollexfen.

Three months later, in November 1862, John's father, the Reverend William Butler Yeats, died suddenly. As if predestined, young John, at the critical

W.B.Yeats (above) and Jack Yeats (below) drawn and painted by their father when they were children.

*The Middleton-Pollexfen mills which straddle the river Ballisodare. The village was
one of the first in Ireland to be lit by electricity generated from the river.
The Ox Mountains rise in the background.*

moment, found himself the inheritor of a 350-acre farm in County Kildare.
Thus he was able to return to Sligo to claim his bride. Ambitious for their
daughter's welfare, the Pollexfen family willingly approved her alliance with
the brilliant landowning young lawyer of such respectable background. Accordingly, John Yeats and Susan Pollexfen were married in St John's Church,
Sligo (now St John's Cathedral) on 10 September 1863.

Now a solidly-serious businessman in full support of the Church of Ireland-
oriented social structure of Sligo, William Pollexfen, from the respectability
of his house in Wine Street, and later in Union Place, was soon to be faced
with the fecklessness of his new son-in-law. The young Mr and Mrs John B.
Yeats returned to Dublin, where John's legal activities became more and more
erratic. In the Four Courts, his concentration too often wandered from the
business of litigation. Idly, he doodled. A little less idly he made sketches,
comic and serious, of judges and of counsel. Frequently it occurred to him that
he had chosen the wrong profession.

Meantime two children had been born. William Butler Yeats, the third,
(1865-1939), 'Willie' or W.B., the future poet, and Susan Mary (1866-1949),
known as Lily.

Sligo sometimes claims to be the birthplace of W.B. Yeats but the poet was
born in Dublin, at 5, Sandymount Avenue (known also as 1, George's Ville),
a semi-detached Georgian villa near the Royal Dublin Society in Ballsbridge.
There is a plaque on the house proclaiming its distinction.

Perhaps John B. Yeats, inheritor of that farm in County Kildare, overesti-

Horse traffic passing beneath the cable cars which conveyed the products of the Middleton-Pollexfen mills on the left to the railway siding on the right.

mated his means. At any rate, recklessly and against the sounder judgement of his in-laws, the Pollexfens, he gave up his legal career in 1867 at the age of twenty-eight and emigrated with his young family to London in the hope of becoming a successful painter. As with the law, his fecklessness showed through again. Intellectualism and philosophising ate into his time and money until the dependance of his family upon the Pollexfens became all too real. With two more children, Elizabeth Corbet (1868-1940), known as Lollie, and Robert Corbet (1870-1873), known through his brief life as Bobbie, the disillusioned Mrs John B. Yeats found herself and her family living for long periods with her parents in Sligo, while her husband fended for himself in London. Such instability might easily have led to a broken marriage but for the timid tolerance and constancy of the ever-patient Susan Yeats.

Through an accident of fate, and the comings and goings of the family across the Irish Sea, Jack Yeats (1871-1957) happened to be born in London, something which, given the choice, he might well have desired otherwise. He never exerted himself to correct those left with the mistaken impression that, because of his total dedication to Sligo, he must surely have been born there. The last of the family of six was Jane Grace (1875-1876), whose life was even briefer than her brother Bobbie's.

Despite his neglect of practicalities, John Butler Yeats imbued his children with his own artistic sensitivity and intellectualism. He encouraged them to

*Susan Yeats née Pollexfen
(1841-1900), mother of W.B.,
Jack, Lily and Lolly.*

take an interest in literature and the arts. In his *Reveries Over Childhood and Youth* Willie tells of that muddy, tidal area just outside Sligo, on the left of the Rosses Point road, an unattractive place where dead horses were buried. There, sitting in the bent grass, at the age of eight or nine, his father read him the *Lays of Ancient Rome*, 'the first poetry that had moved me after the stable-boy's Orange rhymes.' Later, perhaps because of Willie's lively reaction, he read him *Ivanhoe* and *The Lay of the Last Minstrel*.

William Pollexfen's sense of business had brought its rewards. He moved to Merville, a gracious house on an elevated site with views of Ben Bulben and Knocknarea. It is now part of Nazareth House, a home for geriatrics. At Merville, in addition to his milling interests, he farmed sixty acres. And here his wife, Elizabeth, presided over a warmly hospitable household where she made her Yeats grandchildren feel truly at home. Of their grandfather, they stood in awe, even in fear, all except Jack. Inclined to silent severity, the old man's mind was mostly concerned with making more money.

William Pollexfen never asked a worker to do something he wouldn't do himself. An expert seaman, he once took command of one of his own ships in

John Butler Yeats (1839-1922), father of W.B., Jack, Lily and Lolly.

an emergency. She had hit some rocks in Sligo Bay, and although he managed to save all his passengers, and most of his crew, eight men were drowned. Ever after, the tragedy lived with him. Willie's awe of his grandfather was tempered with a youthful admiration for his courage:

> Old merchant skipper that leaped overboard
> After a ragged hat in Biscay Bay;
> You most of all, silent and fierce old man,
> Became the daily spectacle that stirred
> My fancy, and set my boyish lips to say,
> 'Only the wasteful virtues earn the sun.'

Their grandfather Pollexfen's calculated coldness towards the Yeats children may have derived from his dislike of their father's shiftless life. He had believed his daughter was marrying a man with professional prospects, but time had proved otherwise. Life in London was dismal, so harsh indeed that sometimes even food was scarce. Once Willie had to borrow three shillings to buy food for guests foolishly invited by his father.

Like the Pollexfens, Susan Yeats disliked her husband's lassitude. But the faults weren't all his. Brought up with servants always to hand, she was a poor housekeeper. Inevitably, the marriage tottered to a state of mutual indifference, and eventually to the breakdown of her health. Susan's Sligo childhood had left her with a passionate love of nature, something she passed on to her children. But her Pollexfen blood stifled affection. For this they turned to the warmth of their grandmother in Sligo.

THE MAGIC OF SLIGO

As far as the Yeats children were concerned, they would happily have stayed at Merville for ever. As well as love, it had everything to attract youngsters: gardens and open fields, horses and dogs, and a phaeton to ride to the seaside. The boys had a freedom never known in London: woods to be explored, seas and lakes to be fished, mountains to be climbed. And always there was the welcome reassurance of Grandma and Merville to come back to. Is it any wonder that in time to come the Yeats brothers would each attribute his own artistic spirituality to the magic of childhood days in Sligo?

In his overwhelming enthusiasm, Willie often got himself into trouble, as when he was saturated with seawater when boating in Sligo Bay. To save him from pneumonia, a pilot in Rosses Point gave him a slug of raw whisky. All the way back to Sligo on a side-car, and through the streets to Merville, he disgraced his uncle by shouting out to passers-by 'I'm drunk, I am. I'm drunk.'

During one long holiday Willie's Pollexfen aunts decided to curb his gallivanting by introducing a little light education. His response disappointed them. This led to an insistence on a more serious approach. Eventually their harshness in undertaking his early education aroused his father's resentment. 'That tarmagant!' he called his sister-in-law, Agnes, afterwards Mrs Robert Gorman of Sligo. He immediately ordered Willie back to London where he himself could oversee the young man's intellectual development.

Hating London, where he felt himself an Irish stranger, and yearning for Sligo, Willie wrote in his *Reveries*: 'I longed for a sod of earth from some field I knew, something of Sligo to hold in my hand. It was some old race instinct like that of a savage, for we had been brought up to laugh at all display of emotion. Yet it was our mother, who would have thought its display a vulgarity, who kept alive that love.'

Susan and Elizabeth Corbet Yeats - Lily and Lolly - sisters of W.B. Yeats. Later they ran the Cuala Press publishing house.

Jack Yeats fared better with his Sligo relatives. Indeed, Willie complained that his young brother had supplanted him in his grandmother's affections. More importantly, it was in his grandfather's estimation that Jack made his greater hit. Unlike all the others, he could do no wrong. In 1879 he didn't return to London with the family. Instead, he took the place in Merville of the Pollexfen children who had married or moved away. There he was indulged, like a new and an only child, yet never spoiled. From there he went to school in Sligo for the next eight years, first to a private school run by three gentlewomen, and then to Eades School, later to become the Grammar School. He wasn't even taken to task for being always at the bottom of his class. It wasn't his fault, his grandmother contended. 'He is too kind-hearted to pass the other boys.' His father once rejoiced that 'Latin and Greek and learning never affected Jack, since by the mercy of God he never paid any attention to them.'

Unlike Willie's, Jack's gallivanting wasn't curbed. The educationally-minded Pollexfen aunts had departed the scene, and his grandparents allowed him every freedom. He moved eagerly amongst the plain people of Sligo - the farmers, the sailors, the pilots, the jockeys, the three-card tricksters at the Hazelwood races, the clowns and the tumblers who by day erected the circus Big Top on the old Fair Green. His long stay in Sligo repaid him manifold in later life. Above all, it taught him the common touch, something in direct contrast to his brother's off-putting artistic *hauteur*. Not that Willie didn't try - as when he shared his Christmas dinner in the harness room with the man who trained his uncle's horses. But Willie was born 'grand.'

Jack Yeats absorbed the magic of Sligo. Its heathered mountains, its idyllic woods, its islanded lakes, and most particularly, its ever-changing skies were to appear again and again in his future work. 'Sligo was my school,' he wrote, 'and the sky above it.' Indeed, it was there he first showed his precocious talent for drawing, and incidentally, for writing plays - a life-long passion. They had titles like *James Flaunty or The Terror of the Western Seas* and *The Bosun and the Bob-Tailed Comet*. As subjects for painting, he once said the most stirring sights in the world are a man ploughing and a ship at sea. I am happy to possess a little picture of his with a ship at sea. When I look at it nostalgically, I remember his words: 'From the beginning of my painting life, every painting which I have made has somewhere in it a thought of Sligo.'

Some of his pictures had a special significance for Jack Yeats, like one he called *Leaving the Far Point*. It commemorates a visit to Sligo with his wife, Mary Cottenham Yeats - known as Cottie - at some date between 1900 and 1910. It particularly commemorates a walk at Rosses Point with his uncle, George Pollexfen, who carries a stick, and with Cottie. Jack has included himself, wearing a wide-brimmed hat. Of such sentimental value was this picture that he gave it to Cottie on her birthday in 1947. After her death it came back to him as part of her estate. In 1954 he presented it to the Mayor in the name of the citizens of Sligo. Part of his letter reads:

> It has been said that I spent my boyhood in Sligo, and when I left it was to be a student of art far away. That is true, and also it is true that for the next twenty years I spent every summer at Rosses Point, that Garavogue Gateway to the beautiful, old, ever active and intelligent, ever lovely, and ever young, City of Sligo.

Leaving the Far Point is now part of the permanent collection of Yeats pictures to be seen in the Sligo Museum and Art Gallery in Stephen Street.

Chapter 11

'A Tongue to the Sea Cliffs'

THE POLLEXFENS

William Pollexfen increased his affluence when Messrs Pollexfen and Middleton founded the Sligo Steam Navigation Company. Eventually they had some twenty ships plying between Sligo and various English, Welsh and Scottish ports, as well as some in continental Europe. The better to check on the movements of his fleet, William Pollexfen had an observation post built on the roof of the company's Sligo office at the corner of Wine Street and Adelaide Street. The structure is still in position. He left Merville to live in Charlemont House because it commanded a view of the entire harbour area. Thus he could work himself into a white rage when the filthy smoke of a steamer betrayed the use of cheap coal.

Voyaging between Liverpool and Sligo on one of his grandfather's ships was one of Willie's great delights. He boasted to other boys about it, but never mentioned his sea-sickness. Always he remembered 'the look of the great cliffs of Donegal, and Tory Island men coming alongside with lobsters, talking Irish and, if it was night, blowing on a burning sod to draw our attention.'

As age curtailed William Pollexfen's activities, his son, George, the Yeats brothers' favourite uncle, was recalled from Ballina. A bundle of contradictions, he was reputed to be the greatest horseman in Connaught, as well as being a namby-pamby hypochondriac. He had a second-sighted servant called Mary Battle who was a goldmine of supernatural lore for Willie, a debt which he acknowledged. George also kept a man-servant to look after his racehorse and the donkey which kept it company. For economy, freedom and peace, Willie spent long holidays with his uncle George at his home in Sligo, Thornhill, the second of a pair of semi-detached houses beyond the railway bridge on the Sligo-Strandhill road, or at his seaside house, Moyle Lodge in Rosses Point.

Meantime, William Pollexfen had taken to building his own tomb in St John's Churchyard. He could have shared with his partner in the Middleton tomb, but he complained: 'I am not going to lie with those old bones.' Being a newcomer to Sligo, he had to prepare a family resting place. Every day he walked to St John's to supervise the work. In due course all was ready, with the name Pollexfen in large gilt letters at the top of the new headstone over the empty, waiting tomb.

Left: William Pollexfen (1816-1892), the maternal grandfather of W.B.Yeats. Opposite: His maternal grandmother, Elizabeth Pollexfen (1819-1892).

Aged sixteen in 1887, Jack Yeats left his grandparents in Sligo to study art in London. They moved to a smaller house, their last home. Called Rathedmond, it stood opposite George's house on the Strandhill road.

William and Elizabeth Pollexfen died in 1892 within six weeks of one another. On the right of the drive, near the main entrance to St John's Cathedral, their tombstone reads:

> *Elizabeth Pollexfen*
> *Died 2nd October, 1892*
> *Aged 73 years*
> *William Pollexfen*
> *Died 12th November, 1892*
> *Aged 81 years*

The Pollexfen dynasty in Sligo lasted a brief one hundred years. The birth of Charles, their first son, coincided with the coronation of Queen Victoria in 1838. Isabella, the last of the Sligo Pollexfens, died in 1938.

John Butler Yeats claimed that, by marriage with a Pollexfen, he had given

a tongue to the sea cliffs. True, if untrammelled imagination came from Yeatsian blood, that coming from the Pollexfens stamped the stability on the brothers that enabled them to stay the course - unlike their well-meaning father. Uncertain that, for his part, he had the approval of his ancestors, Willie begs them, now 'spiritualised by death,' to judge his work:

> I call on those who call me son,
> Grandson, or great-grandson,
> On uncles, aunts, great-uncles or great-aunts,
> To judge what I have done.
> Have I, that put it into words,
> Spoilt what old loins have sent?
> Eyes spiritualised by death can judge,
> I cannot, but I am not content.
> He that in Sligo at Drumcliff
> Set up the old stone cross,
> That red-headed rector in County Down,
> A good man on a horse,
> Sandymount Corbets, that notable man
> Old William Pollexfen,
> The smuggler Middleton, Butlers far back,
> Half legendary men.

Through the '90s and the first decade of this century, both Willie and Jack Yeats spent summers with their uncle George Pollexfen at Thornhill in Sligo, or at Moyle Lodge in Rosses Point. A unique relationship grew between Willie and his old uncle. They each discovered they were 'strangely beset by the romance of Ireland.' As well, probably from long association with his second-sighted servant, Mary Battle, George was preoccupied with the supernatural.

At Rosses Point they made experiments in thought transference. Willie would walk on the seashore, George on the cliff-top. Without speaking, Willie would imagine a symbol, while George noted what passed before his own mind's eye. Soon George had acquired a facility, never failing to see the appropriate vision first thought up by Willie. At night they both concentrated an agreed symbol on the sleeping Mary Battle. Next morning as she served breakfast they'd enquire what she had dreamt. The result might be a crude version of their symbol, as when they had chosen an allegorical marriage of Heaven and Earth, and Mary Battle's dream turned up as the marriage of the Roman Catholic bishop of Elphin to 'a very high up lady.'

Everything described by the priests in their sermons in Sligo Cathedral was seen afterwards by Mary Battle, including the gates of Purgatory. As for the fairies, they were small fry, always recognisable to her by their signature tune, *'The Distant Waterfall.'* More important was her vision of Queen Maeve, whom she saw through the window at Moyle Lodge coming through the air over the mountains and the sea straight to Rosses Point.

Willie recorded Mary's description of the Queen: 'She had no stomach on her but was slight and broad in the shoulders, and was handsomer than anyone you ever saw.' Apparently, she was accompanied by a chorus of other women, some in long white dresses with their hair down, and some in short dresses with their hair up. They were fine and dashing, 'like the men that do be riding their horses in twos and threes on the slopes of the mountains with their swords swinging.'

Down the road from Moyle Lodge, near the Rosses Point pilot house, the Master Pilot one night met 'a procession of women in what seemed the costume of another age.' Willie wondered if they were people of the past revisiting the places where they had lived. With hindsight his naïvety seems absurd.

The youthful Yeats was first caught up in the web of the supernatural, as I was years later, because of the conviction with which their ghost stories were told by the people of Sligo. But, his interest roused, Yeats was to pursue his curiosity by joining in the spiritualism of Madame Blavatsky's circle in London in their shuddering exploration of the secrets of the other world.

His mastery of the macabre is shown to good effect in *The Words Upon the Window-Pane*, his play on spiritualism written in 1934 at Coole, County Galway, the home of Lady Gregory, his friend and mentor. Notwithstanding the magnitude of the ghostly population of Ireland, Yeats finds it necessary to make one character say: 'This country is still sufficiently medieval to make spiritualism an undesirable theme for gossip.' Later the trance-medium herself remarks: 'We were all sceptics once.' I like to think that, but for his Sligo background, Yeats could never have generated that sense of ghostly *frisson* that comes when Mrs Henderson, the medium in the play, now fully awake, is suddenly possessed by the spirit of Jonathan Swift.

Not even the death of George Pollexfen in 1910 severed the Yeatsian links with Sligo. Of course it meant fewer visits, but to the ends of their lives nothing was ever to diminish the brothers' love of the place, nor to lessen their grateful memories of their mother's people, the Pollexfen family. For as long as poetry is read, that family will have its place in English literature:

> Five-and-twenty years have gone
> Since old William Pollexfen
> Laid his strong bones down in death
> By his wife Elizabeth
> In the grey stone tomb he made.
> And after twenty years they laid
> In that tomb by him and her
> His son George, the astrologer;
> And Masons drove from miles away
> To scatter the Acacia spray
> Upon a melancholy man
> Who had ended where his breath began.

The poem goes on to mourn the deaths of other members of the Pollexfen family, ending:

> At all these death-bed women heard
> A visionary white sea-bird
> Lamenting that a man should die;
> And with that cry I have raised my cry.

The homes of the Yeats relatives in and around Sligo were neither large nor distinguished, least of all in the beauty of their architecture. Mostly they were cosy, modest houses. But then Sligo town (now Sligo city) itself isn't noteworthy for its architecture. Indeed, Seán O Faolain recorded a critical note for historians of architecture: 'Do not on any account miss Sligo. It is nineteenth century macaroni' - a harsh judgement, considering that any claims to beauty made by Sligo are made for its surroundings rather than for the town itself.

The house in Wine Street, William Pollexfen's first Sligo home, with its conspicuous watch-tower, was clearly designed for business rather than for residential purposes. His second home was a small house in Union Place, a narrow street. Merville squats, a plain, square, stone building now overshadowed by Nazareth House to which it is linked. The surrounding trees and the more distant mountains still lend an enchantment.

Willie's grand-aunt, Micky (Mary Yeats 1821-1891), a life-long farmer, lived in a small two-storeyed house called Seaview on the right of the Sligo-Rosses Point road. Covered with creepers, it looked out on a garden with big box borders. There for the first time he saw 'the crimson streak of the gladiolus.'

Beside the Borough Boundary stone on the old Sligo-Bundoran road is the elaborately-named Fort Louis at Rathbraughan, a long single storeyed house on the Rathbraughan river, the home of Willie's granduncle, Matthew Yeats (1819-1885). From Merville to this house he often rode his red pony, and in the little river nearby he sailed the toy boats fashioned for him by pilots and sailors in deference to the status of his grandfather.

ELSINORE AND AVENA

At Rosses Point there are several family-associated houses. I have already mentioned Moyle Lodge, where the Yeats brothers spent their summers up to the death of George Pollexfen in 1910. Next door was Bawnmore Lodge, once a Middleton family house. Both lodges stand close to the entrance to Elsinore Lodge which overlooks the little fishing harbour of Rosses Point. Built by John Black, a successful Sligo smuggler, it was purchased by the Middleton family in 1867, together with the entire promontory lying between the Sligo Channel and the Drumcliff estuary, for the sum of £17,500. Commanding the sound between Rosses Point and Coney Island, once a smuggler's paradise, Elsinore Lodge was so named by somebody familiar with the siting of the Danish royal castle of Elsinore which commands the Kattegat, the sound between Denmark and Sweden.

With their Middleton cousins, Willie and Jack Yeats spent many an enchanting summer's day boating, swimming, fishing or lounging at Elsinore Lodge. Yeats has given the house its place in literature:

> My name is Henry Middleton,
> I have a small demesne,
> A small forgotten house that's set
> On a storm-bitten green.

I scrub its floors and make my bed,
I cook and change my plate,
The post and garden-boy alone
Have keys to my old gate.

Sadly, Elsinore is now worse than a 'forgotten house'. It is a revolting piece of wreckage, as truly destroyed as if it had suffered a bombardment from the smugglers' guns which once graced its lawns to command the Sligo estuary. In its hey-day it was believed by the Middletons to be haunted by the ghosts of smugglers who sometimes tapped on the window panes.

Avena, a house near the Middleton and Pollexfen Flour Mills in Ballisodare, five miles south of Sligo, was the home of the Yeats brothers' great-uncle, William Middleton. He spent the winter at Ballisodare and the summer at Rosses Point. Said, of course, to be haunted, it was another of the Sligo family houses which influenced Willie, the Middletons being great people for country stories. In *Reveries* he admits his debt: 'The first faery stories that I heard were in the cottages about their houses.' The Middletons had no 'edge' to them. As Willie put it, they 'took the nearest for friends and were always in and out of the cottages of pilots and tenants.'

Still further out, some eight miles from Sligo, Willie would sometimes ride to Castle Dargan, between Collooney and Ballygawley, 'where lived a brawling squireen, married to one of my Middleton cousins.' In *Reveries* he continues: 'It was, I dare say, the last household where I could have found the reckless Ireland of a hundred years ago in final degradation. But I liked the place for the romance of its two ruined castles facing one another across a little lake, Castle Dargan and Castle Fury.'

A story I often heard as a child concerned empty mansions or ruined castles seen to be brilliantly lit at dead of night, with a crowded old-fashioned ball in progress. A man I knew told of seeing such a sight through an east window of the house of people whom we knew. Like all 'big houses' in County Sligo, it was haunted, this time by a bigoted forbear reputed to have desecrated a holy well.

My mother and her sister were guests in that house, occupying the bedroom with the east window. During the night they were wakened, not by a noise but by the feeling of a presence. Silently, a figure had opened the door, moving noiselessly by the foot of the bed towards the east window. An outline, visible even in the dark, it stood looking through the window for a few minutes. Then, as silently as before, it slowly retreated, closing the bedroom door without making the slightest sound.

Early next day my mother and my aunt found an excuse to leave immediately for home. Both were solid, sensible, professional and mature English women, in no way given to the ghostly cult of County Sligo. In fact they resented and ridiculed it, if only because it instilled in children a terror of the dark. However, they both found it difficult to rationalise that particularly creepy experience.

Yeats had heard something similar about great balls seen by night through the vacant windows of ancient ruins like Castle Dargan:

> O, but I saw a solemn sight;
> Said the rambling, shambling travelling-man;
> Castle Dargan's ruin all lit,
> Lovely ladies dancing in it.

Sligo City.

Chapter 12

The City of Sligo

TOUR 1

THOMAS CARLYLE AND MICHAEL COLLINS

Thomas Carlyle, that irascible Scotsman of English letters, twice toured Ireland in the 1840s, once before and once after the Great Famine. No lover of the Irish, he suggested they 'must either be improved a little, or else exterminated.' Yet he well realised the cause of the country's plight: 'England is guilty towards Ireland,' he said, 'and reaps at last, in full measure, the fruit of fifteen generations of wrong-doing.'

Carlyle approved of little that he saw as he progressed through the Irish countryside on a Bianconi car. He found Sligo, like the rest of Ireland, a place of beauty and of beggary. But Sligo has remembered with gratitude the treasured words, spoken perhaps when Carlyle's transport had reached that elevated point on the Dublin road, near the cemetery gate, from which is seen the wooded valley, its centre the hill-girt town below: 'Sligo, beautiful descent into, beautiful region altogether.'

Carlyle would have entered Sligo by the old Mail Coach Road. Nowadays you enter by what was once called the New Line, or Albert Road until it became Pearse Road, the names confirming William Bulfin's view that there are three Sligos: 'The Irish Sligo, the Ascendancy Sligo and the Sligo which straddles between Ascendancy and Nationalism.' Indeed, where the Mail Coach Road parts from the Pearse Road there stands a First World War cenotaph, probably the only one in the Republic where poppy wreaths may repose in safety. Frank O'Connor called Sligo unique: 'It is the only county along this seaboard which has been civilised ... It has nothing of the smug majority orthodoxy of Protestant towns like Portadown or Catholic towns like Clonakilty.'

Descending to the end of Pearse Road, the first turn right, beside the Garda Station, is Chapel Street, leading to Cranmore, the one-time site of Sligo Jail. Built in 1818, it had the forbidding aspect appropriate to a place of detention and death. Its walls, inside and out, saw many an execution, the last in public being on 19 August, 1861, when five thousand Sligo people gathered to see a young man from Ballymote being given 'the long drop'.

For preaching 'disaffection' at Granard while making an anti-conscription speech in April 1918, Michael Collins found himself on remand in Sligo Jail.

Sligo Jail at Cranmore beside the Garavogue river with Cairns Hill in the background. The area is now occupied by the Cranmore housing estate.

On arrival there he discovered Frank McGuinness of Longford, an uncle of his young friend Brigid Lyons, afterwards the distinguished Dr Brigid Lyons Thornton. On 18 April, Collins wrote to Brigid from Sligo Jail: 'I am looking forward to getting a glimpse of him at Mass on Sunday. It will be only his back though - they put "sentenced men" nearer the altar than those on remand.'

For all their height, the walls of Sligo Jail were crossed by men determined to free Ireland. To me the place was synonymous with the name of Frank Carty, a leader of that noble Republican army which fought the Anglo-Irish War. He was a regular visitor to my father. A huge jovial man, he never objected when the doctor's lad pinched his bicycle to spin up and down the avenue, one leg reaching the far pedal under the cross-bar. After my father's death, Carty visited his successor, Dr Eddie Connolly, who lived with us for a time. On Carty's first visit, the well-meaning new doctor introduced him as 'Mr Brown.' After a stupefied pause, everybody burst out laughing, Carty most of all.

In 1920 Carty was arrested for raiding for arms at Templehouse, the home of the Percevals near Ballymote. As a leader he was of such importance that at 2 a.m. on 26 May 1920, one hundred men surrounded Sligo Jail, broke open the gates and doors and rescued Carty. The county was scoured by the RIC and the military but no trace of the raiders or the prisoner was found. In February 1921 he made a sensational escape from Derry Jail for which he was

Sligo Courthouse in 1910, 24 May, during the Proclamation of King George V.

tried by courtmartial, and so found himself back in prison with a sentence of ten years penal servitude.

From the Chapel Street-Pearse Road corner we go straight on through Teeling Street, so-called after the hero of the battle of Carricknagat (see Chapter 2).

On the left is the Courthouse, a striking-looking building with an octagonal tower some sixty feet high, topped off with an iron finial twelve feet higher. The tower cunningly conceals a many-potted chimney. Seán O Faolain called the building 'a perfect example of Municipal Gothic: crazy from the lightning conductor down.' Solicitors' offices proliferate in the vicinity, an old sign indicating where once practised the quaintly-named legal partnership of Argue and Phibbs.

Straight ahead, and before entering Thomas Street, we meet the Castle Street-Abbey Street intersection. Turning right into Abbey Street, we cannot miss the high-towered remains of the Dominican Abbey, the only medieval building which survives. It is, of course, Sligo's architectural *pièce de resistance*.

Top: Built in 1253 by Maurice Fitzgerald, Lord Deputy and Chief Justice of Ireland, the Sligo Dominican Abbey suffered pillage and fire before its final destruction in 1642.
Bottom: A quiet riverside corner after a snowfall, Sligo, 1950s.

The Dominicans were brought to Sligo by Maurice Fitzgerald, the Lord Deputy and Chief Justice of Ireland, who was also at that time the Master of Sligo and of the surrounding territory. He had first built himself a fortified castle which stood in the vicinity of the present Castle Street, but of which no trace remains. In 1253 he built the Abbey and gave it, together with land extending to the river, to the Dominicans. In 1414 it was extensively damaged by fire. Its restoration, however, preserved much of the original building, until 1642 when it was pillaged and burnt by Sir Frederick Hamilton. About two hundred years ago it suffered greatly from commercial vandalism. Using the sacred edifice as a sort of quarry, one Thomas Corcoran demolished the north and west sides, using the stones to build houses in Thomas Street and Corcoran's Mall, both named after the 'developer'. After the assassination in 1963 of the President of the United States the Mall became John F. Kennedy Parade.

The nave and choir run west to east, the mullioned east window supporting a structure of delicately-cut stone tracery in its Gothic arch, all still in perfect condition. Beneath this window stands a unique feature: the high altar, still intact, with a panelled front, and a covering slab with an incised cross. To the right is the O'Connor memorial erected in 1624, marking the tomb of Sir Donogh O'Connor, Lord of County Sligo, and his wife, the widowed Lady Eleanor Butler, Countess of Desmond. With the crest and arms of the O'Connor family, the tomb also bears effigies of Sir Donogh and his lady kneeling in prayer.

There are eight lancet windows in the south wall of the choir. Two have been closed, one to accommodate the relatively high O'Connor memorial, the other having been obliterated when the eighty-foot tower was erected at the junction of the choir, nave and transept. The nave is partially destroyed. The stone-carved corbels on which the roof beams once rested are particularly beautiful.

Once forming a quadrangle, surrounded by a covered arcade, only three sides of the cloisters remain. Three series of Gothic arches rest on piers, the stone-cut ornamentation varying. Most notable, on the north wall of the cloister, is the projecting stone pulpit resting on a corbel and supported by a buttress at ground level. A passage over the cloister gives access to this unique and perfectly preserved pulpit.

In 1832 the Abbey's walls looked down on shallow pits and scattered bones as the reasonably able-bodied scrabbled to bury the daily accumulation of the dead in the cholera epidemic.Graves became so lightly covered that the odour of death permeated the locality, until the Abbey cemetery was closed and the

An old print of Calry Church, now in the Mall, with the Garavogue river, the old jail and Cairns Hill in the background.

new Sligo Cemetery was opened in 1848.

Despite their vicissitudes, the Dominicans are still part of Sligo. Holy Cross, an imposing church, was opened by them in High Street in 1848. In a little over a century the population had outgrown the building. It was replaced in 1973 by a modern church, its architectural concept far removed from the original simplicity of the post-Emancipation Irish Gothic.

On returning to the Castle Street-Abbey Street junction, we should turn right, proceeding down Thomas Street. The Imperial Hotel still stands on the corner of John F. Kennedy Parade, previously Corcoran's Mall, overlooking the river and the bridge. The Imperial claimed 'the patronage of Tourists and Commercial Gentlemen' - which somehow catches its atmosphere. In my father's time we used to lunch there. All guests sat at the same huge table, with a massive silver epergne between you and the beetle-browed judges and barristers on the opposite side.

There was only one waiter. Called John, at all hours he wore a form of tailed evening dress, silently gliding about the place with a dignity far beyond that of his judicial clients. The puddings he brought always came unsweetened. You had to sugar your helping to your taste, which somehow wasn't the same thing. Upstairs there was a massive lavatory, of which I was secretly terrified. To reach the chain I had to stand on the seat and time my leap to the safety of

Calry Church from the opposite side of the river.

the floor before the noisy Niagarous gush swept me into the sewers of Sligo.

On the opposite side of the street was the Sligo Picture Theatre, where they provided 'Two-and-a-half hours of wholesome Entertainment' for one shilling and threepence. It cost only fivepence to sit on the benches that Dubliners called 'the woodeners'. I saw *Ben Hur* there. Beside the cinema were Miss Robinson's Tea Rooms, very genteel for afternoon tea with crumpets. Strait-laced, with *pince-nez* and a black dress reaching to her ankles, Miss Robinson looked more like a headmistress than an expert provider of what my mother called 'a decent cup of tea'.

Miss Robinson had a pet monkey which, as a treat, I was allowed to visit in the kitchen. It was chained to the handle of the oven door of the range. If you showed it a penny, it would grab it and greedily stuff it in its mouth, only to keep it stored in its bulging jaw. One day I had half-a-crown, a small fortune, which I had no intention of parting with. I wanted the monkey only to see it – perhaps admire it. In a flash he was on my knee and had grabbed the coin and pushed it in his jaw. There was no one to witness my fury, so I slapped his face good and soundly. With a piercing scream he leaped at me, biting my finger with a ferocity that clearly paid a debt of retribution. With a throbbing finger, and the loss of my fortune, I was still more concerned about the beast's give-away scream. So, with a lying nonchalance, I quietly returned to the tea-table boasting that the little pet monkey remembered me. And for many a day I remembered him, never again trusting Miss Robinson's nor anybody else's 'pet' monkey.

Across the bridge and to the right was Gilbrides' Garage - 'Gilbride Himself', as he liked to be called when, seventy years ago, he serviced my father's car. It was a Crit or Krit - I'm sure neither of the spelling nor of the country of the car's origin. What I *do* know is that, being seventeen miles from Gilbride Himself, the nearest garage, our car was more trouble than it was worth. No matter how many two-gallon tins of petrol my father kept in stock, there were emergencies when he had to borrow from Major Clarence Hillas, the only other car-owner in our locality. My mother had a trap, with a piebald pony called Belle. At first my father said he wouldn't be seen dead riding behind a circus pony, but often, with no alternative, he was glad to. Oats for Belle were easier to come by in Skreen, County Sligo, than petrol for the Crit.

Keeping straight on through Bridge Street we meet the T-junction of Stephen Street to the left and the Mall on the right. The tower and spire of Calry Church dominate the Mall, a street of stately Sligo homes looking out on the river. As a boy, Yeats was familiar with one of these houses: 'Sometimes my grandmother would bring me to see some Sligo gentlewoman whose garden ran down to the river, ending there in a low wall, full of wallflowers, and I would sit upon my chair, very bored while my elders ate their seed cake and drank their sherry.'

Originating on the southern slopes of Knocknarea as an Erasmus Smith foundation, Primrose Grange School was united with the old diocesan school in the Mall in 1907, to become the Sligo Grammar School. A one-time headmaster was called Eades. Hence the Yeatsian reference:

Many a son and daughter lies
Far from the customary skies
The Mall and Eades Grammar school,
In London or in Liverpool.

Opposite the Grammar School is Sligo General Hospital. The Model School and the Masonic Lodge both stand on sites high over the roadway. The new Connaughton Road links the Mall to Markievicz Road, and from here can be seen the Green Fort, a seventeenth century earthen fort on an eminence once held by the Cromwellians to command all approaches to Sligo.

Hyde Bridge with the Yeats Memorial Building on the right.

YEATS MEMORIAL MUSEUM AND ART GALLERY

Returning along the Mall, we go straight down Stephen Street. On the right, occupying the old Congregational Church and its Manse, are the County Library, its Art Gallery and the Yeats Memorial Museum.

Dating from the mid-'50s, the Yeats Memorial Museum includes work by the poet's gifted relatives: John B. Yeats, his father who, unfortunately, philosophised more than he painted; his brother, Jack, whose development as a painter complemented Willie's as a poet, and of course, the Yeats sisters, Lollie and Lily, whose artistic achievements in the Dun Emer and the Cuala presses tend to be eclipsed by those of their famous brothers. The Museum contains a collection of fifty-three books bearing the imprints of these presses.

As well as a complete collection of Yeats' poetic writing from 1889 to 1936 (including Spanish, French and Japanesse translations), there are many collections of letters: those of Ethel Mannin, Oliver St John Gogarty, Lady Dorothy Mayer, Padraic Colum (donated in memory of his wife, Mary, who was born in Collooney, County Sligo), and Mrs Victoria Franklin, a sister of Susan

105

Nora Niland, one-time County Librarian, who inspired the foundation of the Yeats Summer School as well as the Yeats Memorial Museum and Art Gallery.

Mitchell, who was a contemporary of Jack Yeats at school in Sligo. The Museum also displays the Nobel Prize medal for Literature awarded to Yeats in 1924.

Countess Markievicz shares a prominent place in the Museum. Amongst mementoes of her is included a remarkable picture by Kathleen Fox, which shows the Countess alongside Michael Mallin at the head of their men in 1916 as they surrender outside the Royal College of Surgeons. I knew the artist whose daughter, Therese Pym, was a contemporary when we were medical students at the College. Thus I can share an interesting fact about this picture. Kathleen Fox painted herself into it. Amongst the onlookers in the bottom right-hand corner, you will see her as, unobtrusively, she looks at you straight out of the frame. She makes real the sense of sharing an occasion.

The Sligo Yeats Memorial Museum, the first permanent memorial to the great poet, owes its existence to the joint authority of Sligo Corporation and Sligo County Council, but the inspiration for the museum came from Nora Niland, the librarian of the time. An inveterate collector of Yeatsian memorabilia, she knew what the Yeats family was all about, and what Sligo meant to

Two views of O'Connell Street, Sligo (formerly Knox's Street).
Top: looking towards the City Hall about 1900.
Bottom: looking in the opposite direction. The one-time
Hibernian Bank is on the left.

each one of them. On her retrial Nora went to live in Galway. She died on 29 December, 1988.

The Museum Gallery (not to be confused with the Sligo Art Gallery housed in the Yeats Memorial building) contains a permanent collection of modern Irish pictures, featuring work by Maurice McGonigal, Paul Henry, Evie Hone, Seán Keating, Estella Solomons, AE (George Russell), Patrick Collins (a native of Dromore West, County Sligo), Nano Reid, and of course, John B. Yeats. But the Gallery's greatest pride - and for which it isn't sufficiently known - is its collection of 27 works by Jack Yeats. The collection traces his development from the early drawings and water colours of Sligo sailors and pilots and stevedores and wild mountainy men with far-away looks in their eyes, through his nationalist period (*Communicating With Prisoners*; *Bachelor's Walk: In Memory*; *The Funeral of Harry Boland*, and the like) to his period of the palette knife and the riot of colour. 'I am constantly reminded,' Willie wrote, 'of my brother, who continually paints from memory the people and houses of the village where he lived as a child; but the people of the Rosses will never care about his pictures.' Today they would care. Like everyone else, they'd care very much.

At the end of Stephen Street is Hyde Bridge, formerly Victoria Bridge. Once called Victoria Road, Markievicz Road runs to the right by the river, leading to Bundoran and Derry. The change of name reflects modern history. Strategically placed on the corner is the Ulster Bank. I remember it when it was bombed to ruins after it had been occupied in turn by the 'Irregulars' and by the Free State troops during the Civil War. When he went to Stockholm in 1924 for his Nobel Prize, Yeats on seeing the seventeenth century Royal Palace, was reminded of Sligo: 'The windows, the details of the ornaments, are in a style that has spread everywhere, and I cannot escape from memories of houses at Queen's Gate, and even, it may be, from that of the Ulster Bank at Sligo, which I have hardly seen since my childhood'.

Opposite is Barton Smiths', founded in 1788, a favourite shop of my father's, where he replenished his fishing tackle and stocked up his cartridges. Across the river is an odd-looking red-brick building with a timbered upper storey. Once the Royal Bank, it was presented as a gift to the Sligo Yeats Society by the directors of the Allied Irish Banks in 1973. It is now the Yeats Memorial Building, the headquarters of the annual Yeats International Summer School. It contains lecture rooms, the Yeats Society Library and the Sligo Art Gallery.

Across the bridge, O'Connell Street, formerly Knox's Street, Sligo's principal shopping area, is to the left. Past the Post Office and Lyons' store and to the right is Quay Street, over-topped by the City Hall, said to stand on the site of a second Cromwellian fort. Captured by Patrick Sarsfield, he so reinforced this, and the Green Fort above Connaughton Road, that Sligo was the last western garrison to surrender after the Jacobite defeat of 1690.

Some describe the style of Sligo City Hall as Italian Renaissance. Seán O Faolain called it 'French Renaissance with a tower like a tumour.' Built in 1866, City Hall houses a register of nearly two dozen men, and one woman, on whom the Freedom of the City, Sligo's highest honour, has been conferred. Cardinals and bishops predominate, but two names stand out: Countess Markievicz (1868-1927), conferred in July 1917, after the ordeal of a sentence of death, commuted to life imprisonment, for her part in the 1916 Rebellion, and Doctor Thomas Rice Henn (1901-1974), Professor of English at St Catherine's College, Cambridge. A native of Sligo, and an authority on Yeats, Doctor Henn was Director of the Yeats International Summer School from 1962 to 1968.

The Assembly Room in Sligo City Hall - then the Town Hall - was the theatre in which Jack Yeats saw his first plays. He remembered the plays done there by one travelling company: '*Called Back* was good, especially when the actor in the fur-collared coat walked the town in the broad noon day. *The Shaugharaun* was grand and *Arrah-na-Pogue*. And there was one play, with a collision of two liners, in the Bay of New York. They had a splendid poster. An indigo blue night sky. The ringing harbour lights of New York ...'.

I hope that play matched the 'splendid poster'. Too often as a boy in Sligo I was deluded by huge posters announcing MONSTER football matches, and MONSTER race-meetings, the dismal reality turning out to be a rainy day in a mucky field with only a strip of dripping bunting to proclaim the monstrosity.

It was at Sligo City Hall in December 1927, I first saw Anew McMaster's *Hamlet*, with the young Micheál MacLiammóir as Laertes. That snow-bound Christmas in Sligo was Micheál's first visit to the Yeats country. The days weren't long enough to see all the places named in Yeats' evocative lines, nor to decide which came first, the places or the poetry. One place MacLiammoir remembered vividly: 'the miraculous beauty of Rosses Point covered with snow that was dyed in the rose and purple of a stormy twilight.'

As an Irish boy of fourteen in London, Micheál had read Yeats' *Ireland and the Artist*, and, although the place of actors in Ireland wasn't mentioned, the book had influenced his life. The actor needed an audience, and audiences were scarce in Ireland, but the poet, Yeats, drew his inspiration from the woods and mountains of Sligo, recording it in a language read by millions. In short, Yeats stood 'with Sligo at his back and London at his feet.' Yet the young MacLiammoir, leaving London, chose 'self-imposed provincialism in serving at the altars of his own land.' It was appropriate that the magic of Ireland's greatest poet of his time should be responsible for the repatriation of Ireland's greatest actor of his time.

Chapter 13

More of the City

At the end of Quay Street, beyond the City Hall, the Garavogue enters the Sligo Channel, along which run the docks. This was Jack Yeats' favourite stomping ground. This was where he made friends with the sailors and the pilots, and where he found the material for his early line-drawings and water colours. From here he often saw such sights as a captain 'roaring on his quarter deck, sailing a three-masted schooner with wind and tide down from the town to the open sea.'

Nor were the Sligo docks alien territory to Willie, only his interests were different: 'So many stories did I hear from sailors along the wharf, or round the fo'castle fire of the little steamer that ran between Sligo and Rosses, or from boys out fishing that the world seemed full of monsters and marvels. The foreign sailors wearing earrings did not tell me stories, but like the fishing boys I gazed at them in wonder and admiration.'

Without Jack's bonhomie, Willie always had to make an effort to unbend. In *Reveries* one detects a regret, even envy, at the freedom of Jack's life in Sligo, and of the use he made of it: 'He spent his free hours going here and there with crowds of little boys, sons of pilots and sailors, as their well-liked leader, arranging donkey races or driving donkeys tandem, an occupation which requires all one's intellect because of their obstinacy. Besides he had begun to amuse everybody with his drawings; and in half the pictures he paints today I recognise faces that I have met at Rosses or the Sligo quays.'

Retracing our way through Quay Street, we turn right into Wine Street. The Harley Street of Sligo, it is also the address of *The Sligo Champion*, the principal and oldest local newspaper. Founded in 1836, it has had a chequered career, with many proprietors, and as many editors. In our part of County Sligo it was known as '*the Champeen*', and was lent around so widely, I wonder how the newspaper ever survived financially. But survive it did, and after more than 150 years it is still a credit to its journalists.

The Café Cairo, now alas, no more, was the mecca of the boys of Summerhill College. Provided you were in funds, you joined the mob there on free days for what was called 'a feed' - a square meal to quench the hunger pains and fill the void that beset you all through every school term.

Jack Yeats loved to depict horses and donkeys at full gallop as he had seen them in his youth in and around Sligo.

RAILWAY COMMUNICATIONS

On the left at the end of Wine Street is the one-time Pollexfen premises, with old grandfather William's look-out tower still perched on the roof. The square building ahead is Sligo railway station, the terminus for the north-western region. For me it was a place of joy or sorrow, depending upon the occasion. If you were travelling, there was the excitement of finding a corner seat, facing the engine, and ordering a tea-basket, which would be handed in at Mullingar. If you were seeing a dear one off, there was the struggle to stifle tears and be a man. As I grew older, shopping expeditions became boring, so I used to escape to the station to watch the arrivals and departures and the mysterious shunting manoeuvres, for Sligo was still a bustling railway station. Pigeons flew around among the high rafters, avoiding the pungent smoke and the hissing steam of the impatient engines. Not even the guard's green flag or the screaming whistles of departing trains disturbed them.

All of that changed with the Civil War, when the 'Irregulars', in their programme of national destruction, burned the station and all its rolling stock. From the ashes a new station arose, with only the platforms covered, so that smoke and steam could escape. Affronted, the pigeons never came back, and the station never seemed the same.

In the heyday of its railways, Sligo was linked to all corners of Ireland. The arrival of the first train in 1862 connected the town with Dublin by the Midland Great Western line. From 1882 the Sligo, Leitrim and Northern Counties Railway connected Sligo with Enniskillen, and hence to Belfast by the Great Northern. In 1891 came the Great Southern connection between Sligo and Claremorris, and hence via Athenry to Limerick and Cork. Incidentally, the line south passes through Collooney and Coolaney, and many a bewildered passenger alighted at the wrong station before noticing the near-anagram. All these lines met at Collooney, sharing the same railroad for the last seven miles into Sligo.

In its slow death, the Sligo, Leitrim and Northern Counties Railway was at first deprived of its steam engines, the nostalgically named *Hazelwood*, the *Lough Gill* and the *Sir Henry*, the last named after Sir Henry Gore-Booth of Lissadell. Demoted for some years to diesel-powered rail-cars, the SLNCR finally closed in 1957. After three-quarters of a century, an era in the history of transport in the north-west had ended.

Since 1975 when the last train journeyed along it, the fate of the Sligo-Claremorris line has been in the balance. Still in position, the forty-seven miles of track continue to rust beneath the wheels of ghost trains, while Sligo, Leitrim and Mayo county councillors try to convince Iarnrod Eireann (formerly CIE) that, with the success of Horan Airport at Knock the retention of this railway is imperative for the socio-economic development of the north-west.

THE ARCHITECTURE OF DR GILLOOLEY

Turning left at the Wine Street-Lord Edward Street junction we proceed along Adelaide Street, which brings us to Sligo Cathedral, officially called the Cathedral of the Immaculate Conception. Sligo is the cathedral parish of the Diocese of Elphin, whose first bishop, Saint Asicus, was consecrated by St Patrick himself. The Cathedral was built in 1874-75 during that over-energetic programme of post-Emancipation church building in Ireland, leaving much of it aesthetically unattractive. Sligo Cathedral has been described as 'a kind of Romanesque combination of the Norman and Byzantine.' Elsewhere it is called Renaissance Romanesque. As usual with Sligo architecture, Sean O Faolain saw it with a humorous, if irreverent, eye: 'The Cathedral is Hiberno-Romanesque,' he said, 'on a basis of Norman overlaid by Byzantine and suggests a desiccated battleship sinking into the Wall of China.'

Across the road is the Gillooley Memorial hall, a recreational centre, built as a memorial to Laurence Gillooley, the Bishop of Elphin responsible for building the cathedral. With a stage, a gallery and an auditorium capable of seating seven hundred people, it is much used for concerts, and for competitions during Sligo's several *feiseanna*. On the hill facing the cathedral is what we knew as the Palace - the residence of the bishop and the parish clergy.

*Lennox Robinson with Lady Gore-Booth about 1953, when he may have been
an adjudicator at Sligo Feis Ceoil.*

Still higher, above the Palace, in the most commanding position in Sligo,
stands Summerhill College, still another creation of the immortal Dr Gillooley.
In every direction the views from this elevation are magnificent, especially on
a sunny summer's day. But exposed to the elements as it is, hell hath no fury
as when the winter wind blows from the east. I should know. Summerhill
College is my alma mater, though it probably doesn't know that. I wasn't one
of its favourite sons. My accent was wrong, and I showed no leanings towards
a career in the service of Mother Church. For such as me they had little time.

There were two teachers whom I remember with gratitude. One was John
R. Tracy who had taught for years in Beckenham in Kent before returning to
fight for Ireland's freedom. Interned in Ballykinlar, County Down, he was
struck over the head with the butt of a rifle and suffered epileptic fits for the
rest of his life as a result. Whenever he had a fit in class, the so-called young
gentlemen would throw open the doors and flee in all directions crying 'John
R. has a fit' - one excuse being as good as another to create mayhem and disrupt
as many classes as possible. Tracy was the gentlest, most understanding and
most communicative teacher I have ever known. His talents as a teacher of
English were wasted on a lot of ploughboys who mistook his gentleness for
weakness, and acted accordingly in class. Loving the English, but hating their

113

'Sligo was my school,' wrote Jack B. Yeats, 'and thre sky above it.'

government, he remained a convinced patriot, and now lies buried in the Republican Plot in Sligo Cemetery.

The other teacher to my liking was a young priest fresh from Maynooth, a modest man, without the usual clerical notions of self-importance. He was responsible for my class, Form 1 B, and when it came to the allocation of classrooms or the like, he fought for the rights of Form 1 B like a diligent TD for his constituents. When I exchanged short pants for 'longers', he told me I had now assumed the *toga virilis*, the sign of manhood, like the citizens of ancient Rome. He had the good teacher's gift of rendering lessons into interesting facts which were that much easier to memorise. Bishop Doorly recognised a man of talents, and too soon, Father Vincent Hanly was whisked away to become his secretary - eventually to succeed him as Bishop of Elphin.

Returning to the Adelaide Street-John Street-Church Hill crossroads beside the cathedral, a short walk up Church Hill brings you to the gateway to Merville (now the Nazareth Home), the one-time Pollexfen home, so well-known to, and loved by, Jack and Willie Yeats. From the study-hall windows of Summer-hill College there was a clear view of the house, but the era of the adoration of the name of Yeats hadn't yet begun. All I knew of the name at the time was *The Lake Isle of Innisfree*.

Jack Yeats had Merville lovingly in mind when he wrote: 'I am back with memory in an old house in that old town ... And every night the dining room,

114

When Sligo swans need to negotiate a weir they take to the street, and, however inconvenient, the traffic stops.

and the passages near it, are suffused with a sweet and comforting smell which permeates no passages now. It is the smell of Whiskey Punch. It was a pleasant house to come home to, up under the haunted trees, from seeing a play in the Town Hall.'

ST JOHN'S CATHEDRAL

Turning back down John Street brings us to the Church of Ireland Cathedral of St John the Baptist, which stands almost back-to-back with the Roman Catholic Cathedral. Richard Cassels, the German architect who designed Leinster House, (the seat of government), the Rotunda Hospital and its satellite buildings, including the Gate Theatre, along with Powerscourt House and Carton House, was also the designer of St John's in 1730. He built it on the site of a former Anglo-Norman church erected by Sir Roger Jones, the principal Anglo-Norman of his time in Sligo. The church was refurbished in 1812 with the intention of Gothicising it. Further alterations were made in 1883.

The clay of the cathedral's surrounding graveyard possesses that peculiar quality that prevents the decay of bodies. Instead, they are converted into adipocere, a soft, waxy substance that lasts indefinitely. The phenomenon accounts for the discovery of undecayed bodies buried in bogs for centuries. To grow yew trees in St John's has meant surrounding their roots with earth brought specially from elsewhere.

115

It's a bargain!

This was the parish church attended by the Pollexfen family, and it was here on 10 September 1863, that William Pollexfen's eldest daughter, Susan Mary, married John Butler Yeats, the promising young barrister, they who were destined to parent genius. On many a Sunday through the '80s and '90s the Pollexfen phaeton arrived at St John's to disgorge a happy family of Yeats children on holiday from London. And in 1892 it was here, in quick succession, they brought William Pollexfen and his wife, Elizabeth, to entomb them for ever near the main gate. As age out-paced his uncle George, Willie watched the slowing process, the disintegration of a proud manliness:

> And then I think of old George Pollexfen,
> In muscular youth well known to Mayo men
> For horsemanship at meets or at racecourses,
> That could have shown how pure-bred horses
> And solid men, for all their passion, live
> But as the outrageous stars incline
> By opposition, square and trine;
> Having grown sluggish and contemplative.

In September 1910, the Pollexfen parents were joined by their son, George, the admired uncle whose death ended the regular visits by Jack and Willie Yeats to Sligo.

Amongst the many memorial windows within the cathedral there is one 'To the late Mr. and Mrs. William Pollexfen.' And on the wall on the left of the high altar there is a brass plate which reads:

To the memory of
Susan Mary
wife of
John Butler Yeats
and eldest daughter
of the late
William and
Elizabeth Pollexfen
of this town
Born July 13th 1841
Died in London
January 3rd 1900
Erected by her
four children.

Temple Street runs from the cathedral to the old Mail Coach Road where we first began our tour of Sligo town. On the right was the Fair Green, now built over, where Jack Yeats found local colour: the cattle fairs, the slap-hand bargains by men with keen eyes, the circus tent pitched, around it the 'circus wagons and disillusioned skew bald horses hiding their amusement.'

In my time in Summerhill College, the Fair Green, alongside the playing fields, was filled with Nissen huts, occupied by the Free State Army. Through the barbed wire entanglements soldiers would reach for our sixpences, obligingly to fetch us a bar of chocolate or a currant bun from their canteen. Occasionally, a renegade would fail to return, leaving the losers figures of fun for those without sixpence to gamble.

On the left of Temple Street is a new complex containing the Tourist Office and the Hawk's Well Theatre, the inspiration of the late Brian Reddan, one-time manager of tourism in Sligo. Called after Tullaghan Well and its associated play by Yeats, the Hawk's Well Theatre was opened in 1982 at a cost of £250,000. With a capacity of two hundred and eighty seats, the like of this ultra-modern, purpose-built theatre is rare in provincial Ireland. Financed partly by the Arts Council, the policy was to let the theatre on a fifty-fifty basis to amateur and professional companies. Now, with a Teamwork grant from the Department of Labour, a local professional company has been launched. With

The 1798 memorial with High Street in the background, around 1900.
The tower of the Dominican Friary has since disappeared.

the intention of producing new plays, the Acorn Theatre Company in Sligo are already poised to emulate their famous neighbours, the Druid Company in Galway.

O'Connell Street, Grattan Street and Castle Street comprise Sligo's shopping centre. Local traffic in these streets is, however, compounded by through traffic from the Dublin route proceeding to the north. Congestion has been relieved since the opening of the 'Michael Hughes Bridge' in December 1988. Intended principally for through traffic, and built near the mouth of the Garavogue, the bridge is named after the local councillor who first conceived the idea.

There is a lady at the Grattan Street-Castle Street junction whose removal might improve both the traffic flow and the appearance of the place. With her drooping flag, she commemorates the Insurrection of 1798, and is in the paltry taste associated with such memorials. Seán O Faolain saw the funny side of her: 'There is a statue of the Maid of Éireann,' he noted, 'which looks like a washerwoman hanging up clothes, having forgotten to bring the clothes line: a munificent Mayor supplied four gas-lamps, as tall as the lady, knowing that future generations would need something to hold on to in the last extremity of

118

their hilarity.' Meantime, the lamps have gone but the lady holds her ground!

Irreverent perhaps, but difficult to disagree with. But lest anyone might think that Seán O Faolain hadn't a decent word to say about Sligo, and even managed to resist its charm, he had, and he didn't. 'So ensconced in time,' he wrote, 'it is a town that could, I felt, wind many tendrils about the heart.'

Chapter 14

The Circuit of Lough Gill

TOUR 3

In each of the tours of County Sligo described in this book, I have taken Sligo city as the starting point. Using the Ordnance Survey map (half-an-inch to one mile), these tours can be varied to suit the time available. The point of these notes is to draw attention to things of interest along the routes. And because, as a beauty spot, Sligo is probably best known for Lough Gill, and its lake isle of Innisfree, we'll begin with the famous scenic drive which circumscribes the lake, and may be followed by the northern or the southern route. In taking the latter we leave the city by Pearse Road. Very shortly a sign points left to Tobernalt. Following the rising road between the racecourse and the cemetery, we reach a lay-by from which can be seen the great arc of Leitrim and Sligo mountains, ending abruptly on the left at Ben Bulben's 1,800 foot cliff-face. Below us is the Garavogue river and ahead is our first glimpse of Lough Gill.

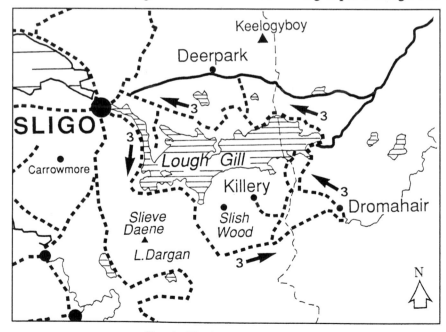

Tour 3 - The Circuit of Lough Gill

Lough Gill under a threatening sky.

TOBERNALT AND DOONEY

Proceeding for about a mile, through a hilly and heavily-wooded area, we descend to a little lake-side pier on the left. A turn to the right quickly brings us to Tobernalt Holy Well. A fern-filled, blue-belled refuge from every wind that blows (see how the candles remain alight), Tobernalt, with its whispering rivulet, is a place of rare tranquillity.

Said to have been blessed by St Patrick, Tobernalt was a refuge in the days of Penal Law (see Chapter 4), when Mass was said there at a rude stone altar. The present altar was built by the Sligo Sisters of Mercy. As children we were told St Patrick knelt at the stone *prié-dieu*. We assumed the indentation in the stone was intended to accommodate the tummy of a very fat man. Pilgrimages to Tobernalt were made on Garland Sunday, the last Sunday in July, and a day which once had a special significance in Sligo. It marked the date after which you could dig new potatoes. It was also the day to cure ailing cattle, or cows from which the fairies had supernaturally removed their milk, by swimming the animals through water into which lumps of fresh butter had first been thrown.

Lady Wilde (mother of Oscar) in her *Ancient Legends* tells of a blind man's cure at Tobernalt. 'Oh look on me,' he said, 'I was blind from my birth and saw no light till I came to the blessed well; now I see the water and the speckled trout down at the bottom, with the white cross on his back.'

Returning to the pier, we go right and at the next T-junction turn left. In a few minutes we reach the car park and picnic area at Dooney Rock. Yeats has been here before us:

> When I play on my fiddle at Dooney,
> Folk dance like a wave of the sea;
> My cousin is priest in Kilvarnat,
> My brother in Mocharabuiee.
>
> I passed my brother and cousin
> They read in their books of prayer;
> I read in my book of songs
> I bought at the Sligo fair.

Several paths lead to the top of the rock. In springtime the air is fragrant with the scent of wild violets, primroses and bluebells, wild garlic also being easily identified. The view over the lake is enthralling. Five miles long by one-and-a-half miles wide, it is surrounded by wooded mountain slopes, and is studded with islands. It is called after Gill, one of the nine daughters of Manannan Mac Lir, an Irish Neptune, who ruled the wind and the seas.

Looking westwards from Dooney Rock, you will see Cairns' Hill above Tobernalt. The hill is surmounted by two pre-historic stone cairns, two cashels and a stone circle. Sadly, that same view takes in a rash of Spanish-style bungalows, one above the other facing the lake. This is something which shouldn't have been allowed by any planning authority interested in preserving the natural beauty of Lough Gill. Nor should a factory chimney have been permitted to breach the sky-line at Hazelwood. There being no shortage of land for the purpose, it is extraordinary how often we allow our most beautiful places to be spoiled for commercial reasons.

About one mile past Dooney we see Cloghereevagh House high on the opposite shore (see Chapter 9). Our road now skirts an inlet of the lake, and facing us is the wooded 970 feet high Slish Hill. Both at Dooney and at Slish there are sign-posted forest walks. For Slish, Yeats preferred a different spelling:

> Where dips the rocky highland
> Of Sleuth Wood in the lake,
> There lies a leafy island
> Where flapping herons wake
> The drowsy water-rats;

A thatched cottage in the vicinity of Lough Gill.

There we've hid our faery vats,
Full of berries
And of reddest stolen cherries.
Come away, O human child!
To the waters and the wild
With a faery, hand in hand,
For the world's more full of weeping
Than you can understand.

In *Reveries* Yeats tells a story of Slish Wood, rather against himself. He thought that having conquered bodily desire 'and the inclination of my mind towards women and love, I should live, as Thoreau lived, seeking wisdom.' So he decided to sleep out, in Slish Wood. 'I could not sleep, not from the discomfort of the dry rock I had chosen for my bed, but from my fear of the wood-ranger.' However, he stuck it out, because he wanted to see his favourite island, Innisfree, 'in the early dawn and notice the order of the cries of the birds.' Next day, having walked thirty miles, he arrived home very tired and very sleepy. For months afterwards, whenever his night in Slish Wood came up, Mary Battle's deputy, a saucy young servant, would break into peals of pointed laughter. 'She believed I had spent the night in a different fashion and had invented the excuse to deceive my uncle, and would say to my great

Lough Gill, looking towards Slieve Daene and Slish Hill.

embarrassment, for I was as prudish as an old maid, "And you had good right to be fatigued".'

THE LAKE ISLE AND DROMAHAIR

Passing between Slish Wood on the left and Slieve Daene on the right, we proceed about two miles to the next cross roads, sign-posted to the left for Dromahair. Nearby is the Cashelore stone fort. Attributed to the Firbolgs, it was vandalised for its stones for local building. About two miles towards Dromahair we meet a sign-post to the left, to Innisfree. A picturesque, narrow and twisty road, edged with hare-bells and dog-daisies, brings us to a pier from which the Lake Isle itself can be viewed. Don't be surprised if your reaction is muted. The island is small - three roods and twenty-nine perches we're told - and crowded with trees and undergrowth. Like a vase over-filled with greenery, it is hidden by the profusion of its verdure. There is a landing place and you can hire a boat and wander happily through 'the bee-loud glade'. And you may even find

Right: Parke's Castle as drawn by W.F. Wakeman about 1880. The castle figured prominently in the war of 1641-52. Below: Parke's Castle has now been re-roofed and opened as a tourist amenity. It stands on the shore of Lough Gill.

Some peace there, for peace comes dropping slow,
Dropping from the veils of the morning to where
the cricket sings;
There midnight's all a glimmer, and noon a
purple glow,
And evening full of the linnet's wings.

Yeats outlived his most famous poem. He may have lived even to dislike it. Despite Frank O'Connor's reminder that Innisfree is also known by the unpoetic name of Cat Island, it is all that the poet claims - with one proviso:

125

if the weather isn't as the poem implies, things may be damply disappointing.

About half-way back to the Dromahair road there is a right turn leading to the ruined church of Killery. This is the site of 'the straining string,' a magical cure for all manner of strains, sprains, pains and aches. Seven egg-shaped stones lie on the top of a flagstone, at the end of which a small rectangular stone projects above the ground. Wrapped around this you are likely to find a piece of thread or string. The sufferer, or a deputy, removes this string for application to the affected part, replacing it with another piece for the next patient. The visitor then says a prayer in honour of God and the Blessed Virgin, while he rolls each of the egg-shaped stones between the thumb and second finger of his left hand. The cure was believed to be infallible. Long-departed emigrants used to send home for 'straining strings' from Killery, believing them to be more effective than the ministrations of American doctors.

Writing of Killery, two Sligo historians give amusingly different interpretations of the 'straining string'. Colonel W.G. Wood-Martin says 'this ceremony at Killery may be regarded as one of the most perfect representations of the survival of the semi-Christianization of a Pagan custom.' Archdeacon Terence O'Rorke says 'the proceeding, no doubt, has a suspicious look, but those who know it best clear it of superstition, on the principle, that the people place all the hope of a cure in the prayers; and a still more convincing proof of its harmlessness is its toleration by the parish clergy.'

Once the capital of the principality of the O'Rourkes of Breffni, Dromahair is just over the boundary in County Leitrim. Battered to fragments in the wars of the sixteenth century, the ruins of O'Rourke's castle were pilfered to build the Plantation castle of Sir William Villiers, brother of Charles I's favourite, the Duke of Buckingham, in 1626. This castle is still to be seen at the rear of the Lodge Hotel. Little now remains of the O'Rourke castle from which Dervorgilla, wife of Tiernan O'Rourke, eloped with Dermot MacMurrough, thus precipitating the Anglo-Norman invasion in the twelfth century. Thomas Moore versified the wretched story in *The Valley Lay Smiling Before Me*, telling of the devastation of O'Rourke on his return to find his castle empty:

> He flew to her chamber, 'twas lonely
> As if the loved tenant lay dead,
> Ah! would it were death, and death only,
> But no! the young false one hath fled.

Moore indulged in poetic license, for Dervorgilla was forty-four - old enough to know better! In remorse she built a chapel at Clonmacnoise, and bestowed her silver and gold on Mellifont Abbey where eventually she died in 1193.

It wasn't the lonesome Tiernan O'Rourke, but *The Man Who Dreamed of*

Faeryland who inspired Yeats when he wrote:

> He stood among a crowd at Dromahair;
> His heart hung all upon a silken dress,
> And he had known at last some tenderness,
> Before earth took him to her stony care;
> But when a man poured fish into a pile,
> It seemed they raised their little silver heads,
> And sang what gold morning or evening sheds
> Upon a woven world-forgotten isle
> Where people love beside the ravelled seas;
> That time can never mar a lover's vows
> Under that woven changeless roof of boughs:
> The singing shook him out of his new ease.

Across the river Bonet from Dromahair is Creevalea Abbey, founded for the Franciscans by the O'Rourkes in 1508. The monastery was accidentally burnt out twenty-eight years after its erection. Repaired and re-occupied by the Franciscans, the Abbey was finally destroyed by Cromwell in 1649.

Following the river Bonet for a mile, the road soon emerges at the east end of Lough Gill, beneath the flat-topped hill, two miles long and half-a-mile wide, called O'Rourke's Table. William Bulfin described the view in *Rambles in Éireann*: 'You are higher up than the grey peaks of the nearest ranges; you are on a level with the others. You are up in the blue air where only the eagle soars and the skylark sings. The rooks and daws and sea fowl are winging their flight below you over lake and valley and hill. Only the clouds lie here when they are lazy or too full of rain to travel'.

A mile onwards, between the road and the lake, is Newtown Castle, also known as Parke's Castle. A strong-house, gabled, with towers, turrets and mullioned windows, it looks over Lough Gill. Wrested from Captain Parke in the wars of the seventeenth century, he received it back, with grants of lands, from Charles II after the Restoration. Through marriage, the estate became the property of the Gore-Booths of Lissadell.

DEERPARK MEGALITHIC TOMBS

Another mile brings us to a right-hand turn, a minor road leading to the megalithic tombs on Colga Hill, visible ahead and to the left. At the T-junction on the Sligo-Manorhamilton road turn left. From Colga Hill the view extends over Lough Gill to Slieve Daene and the Ox Mountains, and the surrounding hilled and hollowed countryside, with the nearby Keelogyboy Mountain rearing to 1,500 feet. Below the hill is the Colga Lake. Once called Giants' Graves and Druids' Altars, there is a collection of megalithic tombs spread over Colga Hill, which have now been dated to about 3,000 B.C. The tomb at the summit is

Top: The Deerpark megalithic tombs as seen by W.F. Wakeman in
his drawing of 1879. Note the broken lintel on the left.
Bottom: The lintel seen in the Wakeman drawing has collapsed as can be seen in this
modern photograph of the Deerpark tombs. Also, forestry has closed in,
sheltering the whole area.

*A sculpture trail
may be followed in the
Hazelwood Forest Park.*

unique for the size and weight of the massive stone lintels used in its structure.

Returning to the Lough Gill road, it is worth taking the Lough Gill loop to Cloghereevagh House. Once owned by the Gore-Booth family, the house is now St Angela's College of Home Economics, which we viewed earlier from across the lake. Church Island is opposite Cloghereevagh. It is Lough Gill's largest island, with the remains of St Loman's sixth century church, and the rocky depression called Our Lady's Bed. Superstition advised barren women to lie in it, turning three times, while praying for maternal fulfilment.

Nearing Sligo, a left-hand sign points to Hazelwood. Designed by Richard Cassels in 1731 for Lieutenant-General Owen Wynne, the descendant of a Cromwellian settler, the square house with arcades on either side leading to pavilions, was built on a peninsula between the Garavogue and Lough Gill. Described in 1791 as 'one of the most beautiful seats in the Kingdom,' the surroundings of Hazelwood House were spoilt by allowing the building of a factory within its demesne. The sculptor, James McKenna, has created a unique collection of pieces which stand in the forest park.

Approaching Sligo, the Regional Technical College can be seen on the right, while nearer the city you pass between the Grammar School on the left and the General Hospital on the right to reach the Mall. You may travel across Lough Gill to Dromahair by the *Queen Maeve* which plies from the riverside in Sligo. The trip provides views from another aspect, and beautifully complements the land route. The circuit of Lough Gill is short in miles, but long in interest. As Bulfin wrote in *Rambles in Éireann*: 'I do not know how many years you could spend going over these roads without tiring of the beauty through which they take you.'

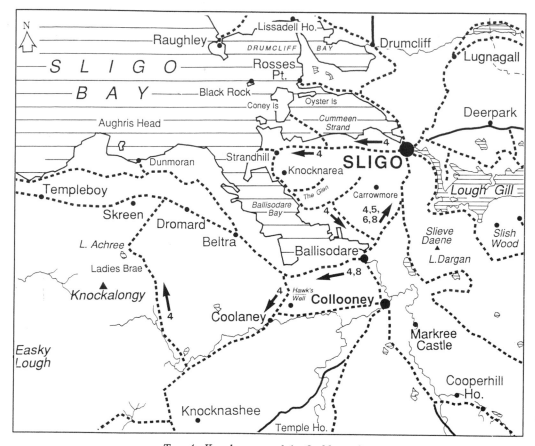

Tour 4 - Knocknarea and the Ox Mountains.

Chapter 15

Knocknarea and the Ox Mountains

TOUR 4

Leaving Sligo for the circuit of Knocknarea, you pass the railway station and the Southern Hotel, going by the Knappagh Road. Beyond the railway bridge you pass both Rathedmond, the last home of William and Elizabeth Pollexfen, and Thornhill, where George Pollexfen was so often host to his nephews, Willie and Jack Yeats. About two miles out, depending upon the tide, the great expanse of Cummeen Strand comes into view on the right, with a panoramic view of Lissadell, the Donegal mountains, Rosses Point and Ben Bulben - provided the weather is clear. Yeats has left us a harsher vision:

> The old brown thorn trees break in two high over Cummen Strand,
> Under a bitter black wind that blows from the left hand;
> Our courage breaks like an old tree in a black wind and dies,
> But we have hidden in our hearts the flame out of the eyes
> of Cathleen, the daughter of Houlihan.

A sign on the right points to Coney Island, and again depending upon the tide, and guided by fourteen pillars set across the beach, you can drive over. Unsheltered from the Atlantic gales, Coney is a bereft and treeless island best visited in high summer when its quiet little beaches are near perfect. It acts as a natural breakwater for the Sligo Channel. Cecil Woodham-Smith, author of *The Great Hunger*, visited Coney. She thought: 'The arch of the sky seems enormous, and the stretch of the ocean immense. Sailing west from Coney the next land is America, three thousand miles away.'

New York's Coney Island is believed to have been named after Sligo's, both being over-run with rabbits. The idea is feasible, for in the nineteenth century there was much traffic between Sligo and north America.

Jack Yeats believed Sligo's was the first Coney Island. In his book, *Sligo*, he wrote: 'New York is in my mind away out there a leap or two over high waves to the west. And down on the shores of our Bay, looking out through the horns of it, with the tall pale lighthouse on your southerly hand, the sun that is sinking wild and tattered here is glistening on the boys and girls of Coney Island - that is *their* Coney Island, not our own, and the earlier Coney Island.'

Having stayed at Killaspugbrone on the nearby mainland, St Patrick visited

Coney Islanders, Dan and Pat McGowan, mending their fishing nets.

Coney Island where there is a well named after him. It is his chair, however, which gets greater attention from visitors. On the bleak north-western corner of the island, facing the Blackrock Lighthouse in Sligo Bay, is what Wood-Martin, the Sligo historian, calls 'a large erratic boulder', pushed here by glacial ice. Coney Islanders contend that it is St Patrick's wishing chair, placed there by the saint himself. By sitting on one of its step-like ledges, you may have a wish, but it is only grantable once per annum!

Regaining the main road we turn right for Strandhill, a windblown village 1,000 feet below the summit of Knocknarea. Close by is Sligo Airport. There are miles of massive sandhills, their pathways patterned strangely by the wind. Nowhere else in County Sligo can the angry force of the Atlantic be seen to better effect. There is an elemental grandeur about Strandhill as you stand between the soaring ocean breakers and the overhanging mountain. You are instantly at one with Yeats:

> The wind has bundled up the clouds high over Knocknarea,
> And thrown the thunder on the stones for all that Maeve can say.
> Angers that are like noisy clouds have set our hearts abeat;

But we have all bent low and low and kissed the quiet feet
Of Cathleen, the daughter of Houlihan.

STRANDHILL AND THE GLEN

Walking the Strandhill beach in a northerly direction brings us to Killas-pugbrone where St Patrick lost his tooth, and where he set up a foundation with Bishop Bronus in charge (see Chapter 2). In a lonely, sandy and wind-swept graveyard there is the gaunt remnant of a church which George Petrie, the distinguished antiquarian of the last century, thought might be the ruin of the original church erected by St Patrick.

The southern end of the beach brings us to the entrance to Ballisodare Bay, where the tide runs swiftly and treacherously. On the opposite side are Skreen and Dromard and Beltra, all part of what was once my father's dispensary district. I remember tragedy striking too often in this dangerous sound when parties of young people, ignoring the weather, would risk the crossing in rowing boats to dance in Strandhill.

Climbing back up the main road we turn right and in a few minutes we're in Culleenamore, directly under the sheer face of Knocknarea. I have happy memories of Culleenamore, where once we took a bungalow. It was down a steep lane, the briars nearly meeting. During spring tides we were cut off, and sometimes a howling south-westerly threatened to make us airborne. But when the sun shone, and the lupins in the little garden stood straight, it was heaven. The seals came out and basked on the sandbanks with an indifferent abandon, though they could make the night hideous with their lonesome barking.

In a few minutes we meet a left-hand sign to the Glen Road, which climbs along the southern face of the mountain, passing the one-time Primrose Grange School, and leading back to Sligo. For its first part the Glen Road runs alongside a deep wooded chasm known as The Glen. Towering to sixty feet of sheer rock on either side, and with tall trees meeting overhead, this geological fault in the mountainside is like some vast over-decorated cathedral, with shrubs, ferns and wild flowers in smothered profusion. This cleft in the rock, walled off from the world, William Bulfin called 'a wondrously romantic freak of nature.' Nor was The Glen ignored by Yeats:

> In a cleft that's christened Alt
> Under broken stone I halt
> At the bottom of a pit
> That broad noon has never lit,
> And shout a secret to the stone.
> All that I have said and done,
> Now that I am old and ill,

Strandhill.
Top: At the turn of the century. The cannon, presented by the Murrow family
around 1900 was - and still is - the focal point of the seafront.
Bottom: Taken in 1952, this photograph shows part of Strandhill village with
Ben Bulben Mountain in the distance.

Beside the last waterfall on the Ballisodare river stand the remains of St Fechin's seventh-century monastery. This Romanesque doorway is surmounted by twelve faces, possibly representing the twelve apostles.

Turns into a question till
I lie awake night after night
And never get the answers right.

Proceeding by the rocky shore we pass Seafield House, one-time home of the Phibbs family, now a burnt-out ruin. In a few minutes' drive we reach Ransboro crossroads, where there is a handsome new church, its foundation stone bearing the name of my old friend and teacher, Bishop Vincent Hanly. Ransboro takes its name from a wren that always built her nest over the local Mass rock near the old chapel. Eventually the people brought the Mass indoors by building a thatched roof over the rib-cage of a whale. Terence O'Rorke, the historian, says: 'under the ribs of the whale worshippers must have felt themselves almost as straitened as Jonah in the whale's belly.'

By going straight through Ransboro crossroads we would pass through the Carrowmore megalithic cemetery, already described in Chapter 1. Instead, therefore, we take the right turn towards Ballisodare. About a mile ahead is Kilmacowen where there are the ruins of two ancient churches, that at Temple Bree said to date from the sixth century. On a stone beside a well, old people will point out the imprint of St Patrick's knees. Yeats laid the scene of his play *The Land of Heart's Desire* 'in the barony of Kilmacowen in the county of Sligo, and at a remote time'.

At Belladrehid there are three bridges where the Strandhill road joins the Sligo-Ballisodare road. Here, at the edge of the sea, we pass fifty feet beneath an iron railway bridge and at the same time we cross an archaic stone bridge, which gave the place its name. It is said to be the oldest bridge in Connaught. Clearly a strategic point, no trace remains of its once impregnable castle.

Depending upon time and inclination, we can turn left, returning to Sligo - only five miles away - or turn right for Ballisodare and include another circuit of Yeats-associated mountain scenery.

Situated at the head of Ballisodare Bay, where the Ballisodare River cascades precipitously into the sea, this village has been an important centre from time immemorial. Overlooking the waterfall, on the left bank, are the ivy-smothered ruins of St Fechin's seventh century church where he also had a watermill and a salmon fishery. In Ireland saints were two-a-penny in the centuries following the peregrinations of St Patrick. Fechin had a brother, Adamnan, also a saint, who lived ten miles away in Skreen. Adamnan often visited Fechin. John O'Donovan, who worked in the ordnance survey of 1836, tells us that Adamnan 'on a journey from Skreen to Ballisodare had his eyes exposed to the influence of the eastern sun and lost his eyesight seven years before Fechin lost his.' The sun shines as fitfully and as weakly in Sligo as anywhere else, so it's hard to account for the fate of these saintly brothers.

The cholera epidemic of 1832 hit Ballisodare so badly there were hardly enough people left alive to bury the dead. In 1833 the great mills were begun. They still straddle the river. In 1856 an explosion destroyed the mills, killing nine. Prosperity was only restored with the coming of Messrs Middleton and Pollexfen. When Dublin was still lit by gas, Ballisodare was ablaze with home-produced electricity from its rushing river.

As a boy Yeats often stayed at Avena House in Ballisodare, the home of his grand-uncle, William Middleton. Here he met the gardener, Paddy Flynn, whose stories of the occult and of the Good People helped to influence his poetic imagination for all time. 'The most notable and typical story-teller of my acquaintance,' Yeats called him. 'The first time I saw him he was cooking mushrooms for himself; the next time he was asleep under a hedge, smiling in his sleep. Assuredly some joy not quite of this steadfast earth lightens in those eyes, swift as the eyes of a rabbit among so many wrinkles, for Paddy Flynn is very old.'

Flynn lived in a leaky one-roomed cottage on the far side of the river where osiers grew. They were used to batten down thatched roofs. Once young Willie Yeats asked the old man 'Have you ever seen a fairy?' 'Amn't I annoyed with them,' was the answer. Another time they were talking of the banshee. 'I have seen it, ' Paddy Flynn said, 'down there by the water "batting" the river with its hands.' One night young Willie, with two cousins, went for a walk. 'Presently we crossed the river and went along its edge where, they say, there was a village destroyed, I think in the wars of the seventeenth century, and

Trees grow from the fabric of the old bridge at Coolaney.

near an old graveyard. Suddenly we all saw a light moving over the river where there is a great rush of waters. It was like a very brilliant torch. A moment later the girl saw a man coming towards us who disappeared in the water. I kept asking myself if I could be deceived.'

Later they saw a small light low down on Knocknarea seven miles off, and it began to move upward over the mountain slope.'I timed it on my watch,' wrote the adult Yeats, 'and in five minutes it reached the summit, and I, who had often climbed the mountain, knew that no human footstep was so speedy.'

With its riverside osiers, or salley rods, it was about Ballisodare Yeats wrote one of his better known poems, *Down by the Salley Gardens*.

THE HAWK'S WELL

Past the Dun Maeve Hotel and over the bridge - which in its blown-up state I remember crossing on planks - we turn right, following the sign for Ballina. About three miles out, at Lugawarry, there is a sign on the left to Coolaney. This road takes us through a wooded gap in the Ox Mountains and down the southern side, past the Hawk's Rock and Tubber Tullaghan, that strange, magical well, otherwise known as The Hawk's Well.

We must differentiate between Coolaney and Collooney, so near are they in miles and in spelling. A MacDonough chieftain of County Sligo apparently

The Hawk's Rock near the Hawk's Well, at Tullaghan, Coolaney.

The Owenbeg river which drains 'the drear Hart Lake' in the Ox Mountains.

gave as a dowry portions of land to each of his daughters, Oonagh and Annie. Oonagh set up house in Collooney and Annie in Coolaney - which goes some way in explaining the curiosity.

THE LADIES BRAE

Just beyond Coolaney village we bear right, taking the road for Cloonacool. About four miles out we meet a sign on the right pointing to the Ladies' Brae. Ascending a wooded valley, with the Owenbeg River tumbling through its rocky bed, we meet an unsigned left turn high in the Ox Mountains. This leads to Lough Minnaun, a little lake my father used to fish, and where as a lad I spent some tiresome times wondering why grown men did this sort of thing. Yeats called it 'the drear Hart Lake', after the family who owned it.

> O'Driscoll drove with a song
> The wild duck and the drake
> From the tall and tufted reeds
> Of the drear Hart Lake
>
> And he saw how the reeds grew dark
> At the coming of night-tide,
> And dreamed of the long dim hair
> Of Bridget his bride.

On a clear day from the Ladies' Brae, there is no more beautiful view in all Ireland. Laid out before you is a composite of the magic territory whose place-names run like a golden thread through the fabric of Yeats' writings. On this high and windy ridge, I think of Benedict Kiely, the writer and broadcaster, who may well have stood on this very spot. 'In the Yeats country in Sligo,' he wrote, 'you wonder which came first: the places that made the poet and loaned him their names, or the poetry that used the places as euphony and symbol.'

Nestling among the lower slopes on the north side of Knockalongy, the highest point of the Ox Mountains, is Lough Achree, 'Ireland's youngest lake', formed by an earthquake in 1490. In the long-ago, and for some unknown reason, an attempt was made to drain Lough Achree. Suddenly a workman cried out that he could see his house on fire in the lowlands. Then every man there saw his own house burning. They hurried home to find, as Yeats says, 'it was but faery glamour'. The lake is still there, but it is invisible from the road. To see the fairy-haunted Lough Achree you must take to the fields on the left to reach the brow of a hill. The lake, dark and menacing, lies close to the sunless foot of the 1,800 foot mountain.

At the bottom of the Ladies' Brae we bear right, following this road alongside the foot of the Red Hill in Skreen, which we'll include in another trip. At the T-junction, we have regained the main Sligo-Ballina road. Here we turn right for a pleasant drive through Beltra woods and Ballisodare back to Sligo.

140

Chapter 16

South Sligo

A tour of the southern region of County Sligo brings us through Ballisodare, turning left beyond the bridge to pass by the battlefield of Carricknagat, and the monument to its hero, Bartholomew Teeling (see Chapter 4). In quick succession we pass under and over railway bridges, because Collooney, once a junction for three railways, stands at a gap in the Ox Mountains where rivers, roads and railways crowd together in their passage from the central plain to Sligo Bay and the city. Bounded on the east by Slieve Daene and Union Wood, and on the west by the Ox Mountains, this is the gateway to faeryland.

The scattered, smoothed rocks in the Collooney Gap are the remnants of the Great Ice Age when glaciers of an incalculable depth rolled on irresistibly towards the sea, scooping out the valley, and leaving great boulders behind. Wood-Martin, the Sligo historian, maintains that glaciation accounts for the availability of the rocks and stones used in later ages to build the massive tombs now dotted about the landscapes of Carrowmore and Moytirra.

The castle, built in 1225, added to Collooney's strategic importance. Red Hugh O'Donnell besieged it, and following the Battle of the Curlews in 1599, accepted its surrender. Terence O'Rorke, Sligo's second great historian, records battles in Collooney in 1291, 1584, 1599, 1691 and 1798. The last battle of Collooney was in July 1922 during the Civil War, some of the casualties of which I well remember.

The village is dominated by the awesome spire of the Catholic church built in 1847 from the design of Sir John Benson, a native of County Sligo. Built in 1720, the church of Ireland edifice was enlarged and improved by Sir John in 1837. Owen Tweedy, whose ancestors owned Cloonamahon and Coney Island and who wrote so charmingly of the island, is buried in the churchyard. The writers Mary Colum and Philip Rooney were natives of Collooney.

We cross the bridge and keep straight on through the village, following the road for Tubbercurry and Ballymote for about two miles. At the fork we keep left for Ballymote. We are now in the vicinity of two of County Sligo's great mansions. Annaghmore, an imposing house in a beautiful demesne, through which flows the Owenmore River, is the home of the O'Haras, a family which for generations has figured in Sligo history. Charles O'Hara, a member of the Irish parliament, distinguished himself by supporting Grattan in his opposition

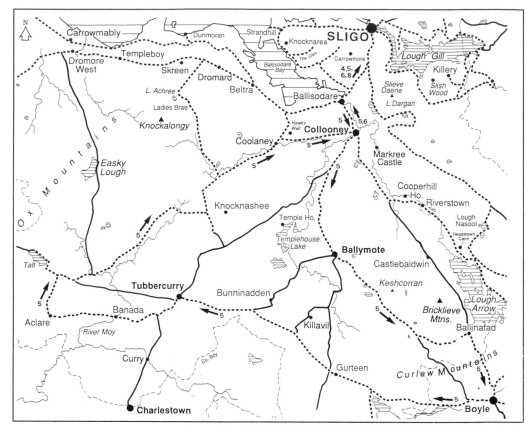

Tour 5 - South Sligo.

to the Act of Union in 1800.

The Owenmore River also traverses the Templehouse demesne, the home of the Percevals. Opposite the mansion is Templehouse Castle, built by the Knights Templar in 1200, and once owned by the O'Haras. It figured in the Insurrection of 1641, when the O'Haras attempted to regain their lost castle

142

and estates. Through marriage the property passed to the Percevals. The demesne, of some one thousand acres, includes Templehouse lake, two miles long and one mile broad. The present vast mansion, built in 1863, contains its original furnishings. It is lovingly maintained by Sandie and Debonair Perceval as a local tourist amenity.

BALLYMOTE TO BOYLE

The chief town of the barony of Corran, Ballymote is noted for its castle. Built in 1300 by Richard de Burgo, the 'Red' Earl of Ulster, its walls are ten feet thick, with passages three feet wide running through these walls giving access to six noble towers. Fought over by the Irish and the English through the centuries, attack and defence left their scars. *The Book of Ballymote*, a 500-page manuscript volume, was compiled in 1391 in the castle. Containing chronological, historical and genealogical tracts relating to County Sligo, the book was sold in 1522 for 140 milch cows. It is now in the Royal Irish Academy. In 1598 the castle was sold by the Mac Donaghs to Red Hugh O'Donnell for £400 and three hundred cows. It was from Ballymote Castle in 1601 that Red Hugh began his ill-fated march to the Battle of Kinsale from which he never returned.

Leaving by the Boyle road, we're soon within sight of Keshcorran, the cairn-topped hill 1,188 feet high, from which there are excellent views. Keshcorran is another Sligo eminence haunted by myth. From the road, a line of caves is visible five hundred feet up on the western escarpment. The opening of the largest of thirteen caves is sixty feet high with numerous internal openings. One cave is said to penetrate for twenty-five miles.

Cormac Mac Art, King of Ireland, was born at the foot of Keshcorran. While his mother was collecting water at Tobercormac (Cormac's Well), a wolf took the baby into a cave - still known as Cormac Mac Art's cave - where it succoured it for a year. The little prince was recovered by using a meat-bait to lure out the wolf. Another cave was one of the many temporary dwelling places of Diarmuid and Gráinne.

The nearby churchyard of Toomore marks a royal mausoleum where lie the kings and princes of Connaught killed in 971 by the Northmen in what O'Rorke calls 'one of the most momentous battles recorded in the annals of the country.' 'The Grave of the Kings' may be seen close to the church.

The name Keshcorran is derived from a legendary De Danaan harper, Corran, to whom the district was granted as a reward for his musical skill. South Sligo still has a reputation for its music, particularly for its unique fiddle playing. Traditional musicians call the area Coleman Country because it was at Knockgrania, Killaville, near Ballymote, that Michael Coleman was born in 1887. The greatest traditional fiddler of his time, Coleman's special style was thought to be lost to Sligo for ever when he emigrated in the 1920s. He arrived, however, in New York in the heyday of gramophone recording. Very soon 'Yankees' were bringing home records of Coleman playing his favourite reels: *Miss Mc Guinness* and *The Reel of Mullinavat*. His technique was carefully studied, and the tradition he had built was revived. He died in New York in 1945.

Beyond Keshcorran, on the left, are the Bricklieve Mountains. Over 1,000 feet high, the summit is flat, barren and boggy. Here is Carrowkeel, the site of another megalithic cemetery, with fourteen burial cairns, two ruined dolmens, and a group of some fifty circular stone foundations which are believed to be the remains of a prehistoric village. Exploration of this cemetery requires time and decent weather.

If we take the left turn to Ballinafad, we pass through the four-mile-long valley between the Bricklieve and the Curlew mountains. Emerging at Ballinafad, we are on the south-west shores of Lough Arrow, a famous May-fly lake between the Moytirra plateau and the cairn-topped Carrowkeel. Built in 1519 to control the important mountain pass, the Castle of the Curlews at Ballinafad features four massive cylindrical angle-towers. Turning right on the main Sligo-Boyle road, we ascend the Curlew Mountains, only 860 feet high. Near the top there are magnificent backward views over Lough Arrow towards the distant mountains around Sligo city.

The name Curlew has nothing to do with the birds. It derives from Coirr Shliabh, meaning rough mountain. Ballaghboy at the summit was the scene of many battles. Two are of interest. In 1497 there was an Irish fight, between O'Donnell of Tirconnel and MacDermott of Moylurg. Not alone was O'Donnell defeated, but he lost the family's treasured Cathach, or Battle Book. Two years later he invaded Mac Dermott territory, recovering the Cathach, which an O'Donnell descendant deposited in the Royal Irish Academy.

The second notable battle was in 1599 when Sir Conyers Clifford, English President of Connaught, marched with two thousand men to take Sligo. Intercepted by Red Hugh O'Donnell with 2,500 men at Ballaghboy, Clifford was defeated and killed. His head was sent to Dublin Castle, while his body was buried on Trinity Island in Lough Key, the lake on the southern side of the Curlews, and which you can see to the south-east.

Passing from Ballaghboy, we descend the Curlews to Boyle in County Roscommon. The Abbey of Boyle, a branch of Mellifont, is on the left of the Sligo-Dublin road. Founded in 1161, it has the largest Cistercian church in Ireland. Vaulted stone roofs still cover the choir and the chapels on either side. In the nave, fourteen carved pillars support arches differing architecturally on the north and south sides. Repeatedly sacked and pillaged, and eventually converted into an Elizabethan military barracks - see the round tower at the

Above: Ballinafad Castle was built about 1610 by Captain St John Barbe to control the Curlew Mountain pass. It was captured in 1642 by the insurgent Irish. The drawing above was made about 1880 by W.F. Wakeman. Right: A more modern photograph.

The seat of the O'Gara family, Moygara Castle, was probably built in the sixteenth century. There is a sheela-na-gig (early fertility symbol) over the entrance.

south-west corner - Boyle Abbey is still among the most beautiful and best-preserved in Ireland. Privately owned by the King family until the end of the last century, it is now a national monument.

In the town of Boyle, overlooking the river - which drains Lough Gara into Lough Key - is the original home of the King family. Designed by Sir Edward Lovett Pearce, the house became a military barracks, and was occupied throughout the Anglo-Irish and the Civil Wars, until the jackdaws took over. Edward King (1612-1637), a member of this family, and a student friend of John Milton (1608-1674), was the inspiration for Milton's *Lycidas*, written in 1637 on young King's death by drowning.

Leaving Boyle by the Tubbercurry road, we immediately re-enter County Sligo, and the one-time O'Gara country. At Mullaghroe crossroads we turn left. The massive sixteenth century Moygara Castle, with its six square towers, once the stronghold of the O'Garas, the Irish chieftains of the area, overlooks Lough Gara and the neighbouring countryside. Further along, by Faleens, the lake and its islands may best be seen. Crannógs, or man-made island homes, dug-out canoes, and bronze objects dating from the early Christian era, were discovered in the 1950s when the level of the lake was lowered. Archaeological research has shown that Lough Gara's crannógs were occupied from as early as 1,000 B.C.

Back to Mullaghroe crossroads and a left turn brings us to Gurteen where there's a memorial to Michael Coleman, 'Master of the Fiddle'. The memorial is flanked by two panels, one reading: 'To the traditional musicians of an older generation who in this area inspired his genius,' and the other 'To those of a later generation who after his passing fostered and preserved that tradition for posterity.' Much came - and still comes - from the musical activity of the Coleman Country, including the institution of the South Sligo School of Traditional Music, attended by many children of Irish emigrants to England.

Founded in 1320 by Edmund O'Gara of Moygara Castle, the six-hundred-year-old Knockmore Carmelite Abbey is at Mount Irwin, three miles from Gurteen. Local tradition claims that, while saying their office, the entire community was exterminated by Cromwell's soldiers, and to this day, near the Abbey, you will hear the monks still chanting their unfinished prayers. In 1987, for the first time in centuries, Mass was celebrated in this ruined Abbey - something which should be encouraged as a step towards the renovation of some of the most architecturally exquisite places of worship which are scattered over the Irish landscape.

TUBBERCURRY AND THE RIVER MOY

Following the sign-posts we reach Tubbercurry, the market town of south-west Sligo. In a reprisal raid in September 1920, Tubbercurry was all but totally destroyed by the Black and Tans. With its population cowering in the surrounding countryside, its main street burnt for days and nights, the gutters running with petrol, porter, whiskey, and melted soap and candle-grease. A brilliant piece of descriptive writing of hell let loose is contained in a long letter dated 5 October 1920, written by Mrs Brigid Gilmartin of Tubbercurry to her daughter, Nora, in New York. The letter is now in the Sligo Museum.

Three miles out on the road to Aclare is Banada Abbey, once the home of the Jones family. Having given two sons and three daughters as religious, the family in 1862 presented Banada Abbey to the Irish Sisters of Charity. For 125 years the sisters taught there, opening one of the first co-educational secondary schools in the Diocese of Achonry in 1958. When, for want of vocations, they left in 1987 they took with them a priceless gift, also donated by the Jones family: a chalice of Irish silver made in 1641 for the Order of Hermits of St Augustine, the original owners of Banada Abbey. Formerly members of the Church of Ireland, the Jones family attributed their conversion to Catholicism to an incident near Banada when a Jones was about to thrash a priest, and his arm became paralysed. They developed a devotion to St Attracta, who did for Leyney what St Patrick did for the rest of County Sligo. In 1864 in Rome, the Reverend Daniel Jones had the feast day of St Attracta restored to the calendar, from which it had disappeared at the Reformation.

*Banada Abbey
stands near the
source of the river
Moy. It gave its
name to the nearby
Jones family man-
sion, which later
became a convent
school. (Drawing:
W.F. Wakeman)*

Banada is prettily situated in wooded surroundings on the river Moy, which rises in the Ox Mountains nearby. A long-time friend of my father's family - a bearded man whom I remember very well - the Reverend James Greer, in 1924 published *The Windings of the Moy*, a collection of articles originally published in *The Western People* newspaper. Writing of the Banada area he says: 'The Moy is the soul of this country, and here at Banada it has all the beginnings, all the quiet pools and sedgy banks, all the deep ways and windings where salmon love to return from their wanderings in the ocean to their old home haunts.' From its rising near Knocknashee, the Moy traverses Sligo and Mayo in four directions: first easterly, then southerly and westerly, and finally northerly, past the banks of Bartragh and the cliffs of Moyne as it pours majestically into Killala Bay.

Beyond Aclare we ascend a mountain valley, the Windy Gap, running between the two counties, and leading to Lough Talt, and onwards to Ballina. Having viewed the lake, made dark by the over-hanging mountains, we return to Mullany's Cross and turn left proceeding through Cloonacool. The road through the Barony of Leyney runs parallel with the rugged southern slopes of the Ox Mountains.

KNOCKNASHEE

On the right is a strange hill of nine hundred feet, which lifts itself dramatically from the central plain near Lavagh. This is Knocknashee, or the Fairy Hill, known to some as Mulinabreena, and marked on the Ordnance Survey Map as Gortnadrass. Mentioned by Yeats in '*The Ballad of Father*

O'Hart', Knocknashee's flat top of one square mile is green and lush and, unlike its neighbouring mountains, is without heather. At its foot are the ruins of Court Abbey, built by the O'Haras in the fifteenth century for the Franciscans. An imposing edifice, its central tower is ninety feet high.

Shortly we come to a sign-post for the Ladies' Brae, and another at Coolaney for Tubber Tullaghan or the Hawk's Well. We have already visited both places, and the shortest route back to Sligo is through Collooney and Ballisodare.

Chapter 17

The Barony of Tirerill

TOUR 6

For a tour of south-east Sligo we leave town by the Ballisodare road. At Carraroe, about two miles out, we take the left fork for Ballyfarnan. In a few minutes we're passing between 'the sweet little wood-embosomed lake of Ballygawley,' as George Petrie called it, on the right, and Slieve Daene, or Bird Mountain, on the left, where a chamber tomb near the 900 foot summit is called the Cailleach Beare's house. Yeats called this legendary faery figure Clooth-na-Bare. In his note to his poem 'The Hosting of the Sidhe' he explains that she 'went all over the world, seeking a lake deep enough to drown her faery life, of which she had grown weary ... until at last, she found the deepest water in the world in little Lough Ia on the top of the Bird Mountain in Sligo.'

Yeats believed the Sidhe, or faery hosts, still rode the country as of old, having much to do with the motions of the wind. He noted that 'when old country people see the leaves whirling on the road they bless themselves, because they believe the Sidhe to be passing by.' Which helps to explain the breathless quality of 'The Hosting of the Sidhe':

> The host is riding from Knocknarea
> And over the grave of Clooth-na-Bare;
> Caoilte tossing his burning hair,
> And Niamh calling *Away, come away:*
> *Empty your heart of its mortal dream.*
> *The winds awaken, the leaves whirl round,*
> *Our cheeks are pale, our hair is unbound,*
> *Our breasts are heaving, our eyes are agleam,*
> *Our arms are waving, our lips are apart;*
> *And if any gaze on our rushing band,*
> *We come between him and the deed of his hand,*
> *We come between him and the hope of his heart.*
> The host is rushing 'twixt night and day,
> And where is there hope or deed as fair?
> Caoilte tossing his burning hair,
> And Niamh calling *Away, come away.*

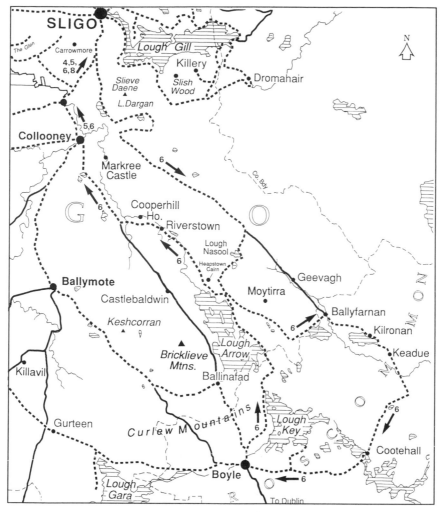

Tour 6 - The Barony of Tirerill

Half-a-mile beyond Ballygawley Lake we turn left. About one mile ahead we come on Castle Dargan Lake, where Yeats 'great pike broods'. A fragment of the fifteenth century Castle Dargan stands on a cliff-top on the opposite side. 'I fished for pike at Castle Dargan,' Yeats remembered, 'and shot at birds with a muzzle-loading pistol until somebody shot a rabbit and I heard it squeal. From that on I would kill nothing but the dumb fish.'

Just beyond the lake we turn right, and after a few minutes on a side-road, right again, passing the gates of Castle Dargan house, now a romantically charming guest house. This was where Yeats sometimes rode to visit the 'brawling squireen'. (see Chapter 11)

At the next crossroads we turn left, re-joining the main Sligo-Ballyfarnan road. About eight miles on, we turn right for Ballinphuill, past Lough Nasool, the lake traditionally associated with Balor of the Evil Eye. The lake is reputed to disappear every one hundred years. It hit the headlines by doing so in 1933, and again, somewhat ahead of schedule, in 1964. One mile ahead, at the next T-junction we turn left, bearing left at the next fork. Ascending the plateau of Moytirra on the east side of Lough Arrow, we reach Highwood and the bleak cairn-strewn battlefield already described.

TURLOUGH O CAROLAN

Descending to Kilmactranny we turn left, past Lough Skean to emerge at Ballyfarnan at the foot of Kilronan Mountain, and a little outside County Sligo. But we have a reason for trespassing! We proceed to the right through Ballyfarhan. Just beyond the village is Alderford, the demesne and ancestral home of the Mac Dermott Roe family, in whose loving care Turlough O Carolan (1670-1738), the blind song-writer and harpist, and the last of the Gaelic bards, spent his final years.

O Carolan died at Alderford, and his four-day wake was attended by ten harpers. He was buried in the Mac Dermott Roe vault in Kilronan Cemetery about two miles further out on the Ballyfarnan-Keadue road beside Lough Meelagh. O Carolan's eighteenth century harp may be seen at Clonalis House near Castlerea, the ancestral home of the O'Conor Don family. Amongst his compositions was the tune later used as 'The Star-Spangled Banner'. Opposite Kilronan Cemetery is St Lasair's holy well, the water of which is reputed to cure arthritis. The lake shore is beautifully wooded, making it an attractive stopping place for a picnic.

One mile past Kilronan is Keadue where annually in August, the O Carolan Festival of Traditional Music keeps green the memory of the bard. As with the South Sligo Festival, Keadue draws both its competitors and its audiences from far and near, at home and abroad. Its raison d'être is a revival of interest in the Irish traditional harp.

We take the road out of Keadue towards Leitrim. After two miles we meet a crossroads where we turn right, bearing left at the next fork. This is John McGahern country, and the Cootehall Garda Station may well have inspired his deeply-moving novel, The Barracks. Crossing the Shannon (there is

Ballindoon Abbey. 'Lame' David Duignan, an eminent scribe, lived nearby at Shancoe.
His writings of the 1670s are now in the Royal Irish Academy. He died
in 1696 and is buried in Ballindoon cemetery.

another and particularly picturesque crossing at the nearby Knockvicar bridge) we ascend to meet the main Dublin-Sligo road near Ardcarn Church. This is the burial place of the Kirkwood family whose house, Woodbrook, is two miles down the road in the Dublin direction. It is the scene of David Thomson's best-selling and charming biographical love-story, itself called *Woodbrook.*

Turning right at Ardcarn we pass by the boundary walls of the old Rockingham Demesne until, on the right, we meet the entrance to Lough Key Forest Park. A visit is imperative. Everything a tourist could desire is to be found here: a restaurant, crafts and souvenirs, forest walks, caravan, camping and picnicing sites. But best of all: you can sail by motor cruiser through the island-studded and historic waters of Lough Key.

Leaving the park we turn right. At Boyle we bear right again as we short-circuit the town, passing the Abbey (see Chapter 16). About one mile out we turn right for Corrigeenroe, to follow a road with superb views over Lough Key and its historic islands. Castle Island was where the *Annals of Loch Cé* were compiled in 1541 for the Mac Dermotts of Moylurg. On Trinity Island are the ruins of Trinity Abbey founded in 1215. This is the burial place of Sir Conyers Clifford, English President of Connaught, who was killed in the Battle of the Curlews in 1599. Trinity Island, or Insula Trinitatis as he called it, had a special association with Yeats.

Preparing for a 'flapper' race meeting on Bowmore Strand, Rosses Point in the 1950s.

LOUGH KEY AND LOUGH ARROW

The last story in his collection called *The Secret Rose* concerns Proud Tumaus Costello and Mac Dermott's daughter, Una, who were crossed in love by her father and his clan. Broken-hearted, she died and was buried on Trinity Island. Swimming to the island, Proud Costello in desolation lay on her grave day and night, calling on his lover to come to him. Then a swirling wind swept over the island, and he saw women of the Sidhe rushing past with Una. Returning in despair to the mainland, he was drowned. They buried him on Trinity Island beside Una, and 'planted above them two ash-trees that in after days wove their branches together and mingled their leaves.' The intertwined trees growing from the lovers' graves lasted until ill-informed conservationists cut them down.

When Yeats was planning his story, he drove from Douglas Hyde's house at Frenchpark to Lough Key, and was rowed up the lake in search of the island where the lovers are buried. He found another island that day, Castle Rock, 'an island all castle'. Its roof intact, its windows unbroken, Yeats planned 'a mystical Order which should buy or hire the castle, and keep it as a place where its members would retire for a while for contemplation ... and for ten years to come my most impassioned thought was a vain attempt to find philosophy and to create ritual for that Order.' Yeats' dream never materialised.

154

At the crossroads of Corrigeenroe we might turn left for a short lakeside drive to Ballinafad. More rewarding is the longer drive by Lough Arrow. To reach this road we go straight through the crossing, and one mile ahead turn left. The route hugs the shore, with the Moytirra plateau rising on the right and the Bricklieve Mountains to the left on the far side.

About two miles ahead, near Inishmore Island, is Ballindoon Abbey, built by the MacDonaghs in 1507 for the Dominicans. Nearby is St Dominic's holy well. Crowned by an unusual tower, the ruin contains a monument with an interesting inscription, and a lavish display of capitals:

Terence Mac Donagh lies within this grave,
That says enough for all that's Generous, Brave,
Fasecious, Friendly, Witty, Just and Good,
In the lov'd Name is fully understood,
For it includes what e'er wee Virtue call
And is the Hieroglyphic of them all.

In the nearby townland of Carrickglass there is an immense cromlech called the 'Labby', or bed. Six supporting stones carry a capstone estimated to weigh over seventy tons. Exactly how these stones were manoeuvred into position remains a mystery.

Across the lake on the western shore may be seen Hollybrook demesne, once the home of Squire Folliott, later to become the Hollybrook Hotel. The story of the love affair of Folliott's daughter, called the Colleen Bawn, was published by William Carleton in 1855, and became a popular Irish love-story, *Willie Reilly and his Fair Colleen Bawn*.

At the next crossroads we bear left. After a mile or so we meet another crossroads which we go straight through to follow the Riverstown road. In a few minutes we're alongside the Heapstown Cairn, a thirty-foot high pyramidal mound of stones covering half an acre, and dating from the fourth century. It is said to be the grave of a High King.

Incidentally, in the Heapstown district, the Conmees were the local family of social standing. The Rector of Clongowes Wood College in 1889, the Reverend J.S. Conmee, was one of the clan. He was the Father Conmee immortalised by James Joyce in *A Portrait of the Artist as a Young Man*.

COOPERHILL AND MARKREE CASTLE

Riverstown is on the Uncion river which drains Lough Arrow, meeting the Owenbeg and Owenmore rivers at Collooney, all three reaching the sea as the Ballisodare river. At Riverstown we turn left towards Cooperhill, a spacious Georgian house built in 1774. Now providing tourist accommodation, the

Heapstown is a great passage grave type cairn whose height can be judged from the surrounding trees.

house contains antique furniture, and even four-poster beds. Built in the days when big was beautiful, Cooperhill is a square mansion rising to five storeys. Legend says it cost 'a tub of gold sovereigns to build.' An ornamental cut-stone bridge spans the Uncion near the mansion, and legend says this cost as much as the house. In fact, the Cooper of the time had to sell part of his estate to meet his costs.

At the T-junction we're on the main Sligo-Dublin road where we turn right. About two miles ahead a large building will be seen high on a hill to the left. A steeple marks it as the monastery of the Passionist Fathers established at Cloonamahon in 1967. Here once stood the house of Yeats' Father John O'Hart. Part of the institution has been converted to accommodate mentally handicapped people for the North Western Health Board. Four sides of the octagonal chapel are occupied by modern stained glass windows.

A little nearer Collooney, on the opposite side of the road, is the imposing Gothic gate of Markree Castle, the home of another branch of the Cooper family. A seventeenth century house, built by Cornet Cooper of Cromwell's army, it was re-faced by Francis Johnston in 1803 in a castle style. In 1832 Edward Cooper, an amateur astronomer, founded an observatory at Markree, where he then employed scientific professionals, making his observatory the most important in Europe at the time. Reports were provided for the Meteorological Office in London, and for Sir William Wilde in his scientific study of

156

cosmic phenomena for the Royal Irish Academy. The Markree telescope went to Hong Kong in 1932.

O'Rorke, the Sligo historian, greatly admired the trees, particularly the collection of rarities, in the arboretum at Markree, adding that 'Markree lends as much ornament to the demesne as it borrows from it.' The Castle took on a new lease of life in 1987 when it was used as the setting for the film *Troubles*, adapted from the novel by J.G. Farrell. Charles Cooper plans to open Markree Castle as a hotel in 1989. Our return to Sligo is through Collooney and Ballisodare.

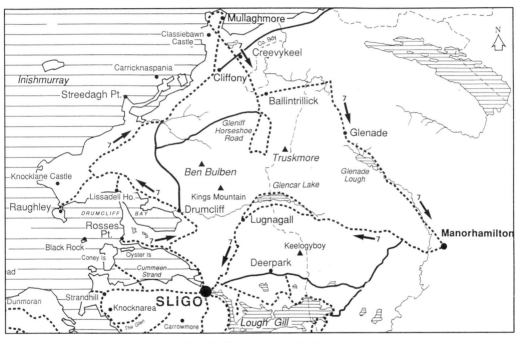

Tour 7 - Northwards to Carbury

157

Chapter 18

Northwards to Carbury

TOUR 7

ROSSES POINT, DRUMCLIFF AND LISSADELL

A visit to Rosses Point is a must, if only because the place was so greatly loved by the brothers Yeats. Leaving Sligo by the Markievicz Road, and keeping left at the first fork, we follow a road alongside the Sligo Channel. On his pedestal the Metal Man - 'the Rosses Point man who never told a lie', as young Willie Yeats called him - points for ever the safest way for ships to negotiate the narrow strip of swiftly-running water between Rosses and Oyster Island. Dead Man's Point, where the Sligo Yacht Club is situated, is where the channel meets the sea. Its name comes from a story of a panic-stricken crew on an incoming vessel who thought they had aboard a sailor dying of a 'taking' fever. Fearing contagion they buried him prematurely, and in case he needed it, they buried a loaf of bread with him. Above Dead Man's Point 'the disused Pilot House looks out to sea through two round windows like eyes.' In *The Old Men of the Twilight*, Willie Yeats tells how Michael Bruen, a smuggler, watched nightly through these windows for the tall French schooner with her contraband to arrive in Sligo Bay. Roofless now, the Pilot House is still there, and through its vacant eyes you can look across the sea to Raughley.

Today Rosses Point is best known for its championship golf course. In Yeats' young days it was a place 'of unearthly resort ... choke-full of ghosts. By bog, road, rath, hillside, sea-border they gather in all shapes: headless women, men in armour, shadow hares, fire-tongued hounds, whistling seals, and so on.' In his *Celtic Twilight* stories he captures the very essence of the wild and lonely desolation of rush-grown, haunted places and the 'Slow low note' of the storm-tossed bell-buoy in Sligo Bay:

> Saddle and ride, I heard a man say,
> Out of Ben Bulben and Knocknarea,
> *What says the clock in the Great Clock Tower?*
> All those tragic characters ride
> But turn from Rosses crawling tide,
> The meet's upon the mountain-side.
> *A slow low note and an iron bell.*

In 1822, with his guiding light, the 12 foot high, 7½ ton, Metal Man was placed on the Perch Rock in Sligo Channel. In the nineteenth century he saw many thousands of hungry Sligo emigrants pass on their way to the New World.

About two miles out on the return from Rosses Point we turn left at the sign-post for Cregg House Hospital, making for Rathcormac on the main Sligo-Bundoran road. Here we turn left again for Drumcliff. Yeats' lines, written four months before his death, pin-point the locality:

Under bare Ben Bulben's head
In Drumcliff churchyard Yeats is laid,

An ancestor was rector there
Long years ago, a church stands near,
By the road an ancient cross.

What he doesn't mention is the stump of a round tower on the roadside opposite the church, a remnant of St Colmcille's monastic settlement founded in A.D. 575 (see Chapter 2). The ancestor was Parson John Yeats, the poet's great-grandfather (see Chapter 10).

The simplicity of the grave of W.B. Yeats reflects his own wish:

No marble, no conventional phrase;
On limestone quarried near the spot
By his command these words are cut:
Cast a cold eye
On life, on death.
Horseman, pass by!

Just beyond Drumcliff a sign-post points left to Lissadell and Raughley. The Lissadell estate contains forest walks and a wildlife reserve where winters the largest colony of Barnacle geese in Ireland. Sheltered by its woods, Lissadell House, which is open to the public, was built in 1830 by Sir Robert Gore-Booth, the grandfather of Constance (1868-1927 the revolutionary, later Countess Markievicz), and Eva (1870-1926 the poet turned social worker). In 1894 Yeats first recognised the spiritual beauty of the Gore-Booth sisters when he became a frequent visitor. At Seville, 33 years later, when he had lost a little of his admiration for the rebellious Constance, he wrote a poem in their memory:

The light of evening, Lissadell,
Great windows open to the south,
Two girls in silk kimonos, both
Beautiful, one a gazelle,
But a raving autumn shears
Blossom from the summer's wreath;
The older is condemned to death,
Pardoned, drags out lonely years
Conspiring among the ignorant.

Leaving Lissadell by a back avenue we emerge at the prettily-situated Ballinphull church, the Gore-Booth burying place. Turning left we leave the sheltering woods to face the bleak peninsula called Raughley. Near that village

160

Lissadell House.Top: The drawing room with its 'great windows open to the south'.
Bottom: The dining room. In 1908 Count Casimir Markievicz, husband of Constance,
painted five life-sized, full length figures on five columns. They included
members of the family and staff.

*Constance and Eva Gore-Booth as children in the
woods at Lissadell, painted in 1882 by the then
unknown Sarah Purser.*

stands Ardtermon Castle, built by the O'Harts, and later annexed by Sir
Nathaniel Gore, an ancestor of the Gore-Booths. The O'Hart and the Cowell
families were intermarried. John O'Hart, a descendant, was the author of *The
Irish and the Anglo-Irish Landed Gentry When Cromwell Came to Ireland.*
First published in 1884, this most useful reference book, particularly for those
seeking their family roots, was re-published in 1969 by the Irish University
Press.

Behind Raughley village is the Yellow Strand, of which Yeats said: 'I have
walked on Sinbad's yellow shore and never shall another's hit my fancy.'
Above the strand is Knocklane Hill with its castle two hundred feet above the
Derk of Knocklane, a semi-circular chasm open to the west where the wind
howls and the Atlantic boils monstrously making a din through which the

sea-gulls scream. The place is haunted by the Banshee Bawn, alias Letitia Gore (née Booth), wife of Sir Nathaniel, a fearless and wilful woman who dressed in white. Once, as an exploit, she forced her coachman at pistol point to drive her round the dizzy edge of Knocklane's yawning chasm above the seething, roaring waters. The performance is repeated by her ghost, her horses now shod with gold. As they say in Sligo, it wasn't from the wind the Banshee Bawn's great great grand-daughter, Constance Markievicz, inherited her boundless courage.

Wild and windswept, the Raughley peninsula suffered from drifting sand which, between 1816 and 1835, covered the land. Lord Palmerston, once Queen Victoria's Foreign Secretary and later Prime Minister, introduced bent grass, thus creating the protective sand dunes which mark this coastline.

STREEDAGH AND THE SPANISH ARMADA

We follow the sign-post for Grange where we re-gain the main road as it overlooks Streedagh Strand and Carricknaspania, or the rock of the Spaniards. Here in 1588 three crowded galleons of the Spanish Armada were battered to pieces in a gale. Hundreds were drowned. Those who reached the shore were beaten and robbed by the Irish. English forces then came from Sligo to administer the *coup de grâce* to any still alive. Lord Deputy Fitzwilliam later reported to London: 'I rode along that strand ... There lay a great store of timber of wrecked ships ... more than would have built four of the greatest ships.' Geoffrey Fenton, another British official reported: 'I numbered in one strand eleven hundred corpses.'

One of the few Spaniards to escape was Captain Francisco de Cuellar who has left an unflattering picture of some of our ancestors whom he calls savages. His memoir, discovered in 1885 in the archives of the *Academia de la Historia* in Madrid recounts his experience at Streedagh: 'I knew not what to do, not knowing how to swim and the waves being great. On land there was the shore lined with enemies who were dancing and jumping around with joy at the sight of our misfortune, and when anyone of our people reached the shore, down on him they came and at once stripped him of every stitch he had on him and then ill-treated him and left him covered with wounds.'

Eventually thrown up on the beach by the waves, de Cuellar with some companions escaped inland where they were sheltered by Teige Óg Mac Clancy in his island castle at Rosclougher on Lough Melvin. Time and the geniality of the Leitrim people changed de Cuellar's opinion of the Irish: 'As to ourselves, these savages liked us well because they knew we came against the heretics who were such great enemies of theirs and if it had not been for those who guarded us as their own persons, not one of us would have been left alive. We had good will to them for this.'

Visible for miles in every direction, Classiebawn Castle stands four-square on a cliff above the Atlantic. From the Sligo-Bundoran road it looks like a creation by Walt Disney.

MULLAGHMORE

At Cliffony village we turn left for Mullaghmore, the idyllic holiday peninsula that juts out into Donegal Bay. Outstanding on the hill, and visible from afar, is the fairy castle called Classiebawn, its towers and turrets high over the sea. This was the holiday home of Lord Mountbatten until that shattering day in August, 1979, when murdering outsiders came and flashed the name of Mullaghmore through the world's media as another Irish trouble spot. Distress and disgrace gripped the villagers, for Mountbatten was their friend, as was Edwina, his wife, before her death in 1960. She celebrated with them in the local pub, as she had mourned with them at their funerals.

Begun by Lord Palmerston (1784-1865), British Prime Minister, the Victorian Gothic Classiebawn was intended for his daughter who suffered from tuberculosis in the days when fresh air was the well-meant panacea for that plague. Palmerston, an excellent landlord, also built the harbour at Mullaghmore, and generally spent his money lavishly to improve his 2,000-acre estate. He built both the Catholic and the Church of Ireland schools, and installed teachers. He gave the parish priest a glebe house to put him on a level with the parson. On Palmerston's death, Classiebawn and the Mullaghmore estate passed to the Honourable Evelyn Ashley, and from him to his grand-daughter,

164

Lord Mountbatten at Sligo railway station greeting his sisters
Princess Alice, mother of Prince Philip (centre) and Queen
Louise of Sweden on their arrival for a holiday at
Classiebawn Castle in August 1961.

Edwina, who married Lord Mountbatten.

Before leaving Mullaghmore we must do a short circular scenic drive round the cliffs, for views of Inishmurray Island and Slieve League mountain in Donegal. We must also see the fabulous crescent-shaped Bunduff Strand, and the little Bunduff swan-lake. Mullaghmore is a boarding place for the five-mile trip to the treeless and windswept Inishmurray Island, deserted since 1948. Once occupied by St Molaise's monastery - or was it St Muredach's? - opinions differ - the establishment was destroyed in A.D. 807 by the Vikings. The island is noted for its great cashel built of uncemented stones, and enclosing a primitive oratory, a small temple, beehive cells and several altars. The 'cursing stones' are said to number forty, but count them as often as you like, you'll never get them to add to the same total.

Terence O'Rorke recounts some other interesting phenomena from Inishmurray. A handful of the island's earth will destroy all the rats and mice in Ireland, or, when thrown into the sea will calm it, even in a storm. If all the household fires went out, a piece of turf placed on a flag in one of the ruined churches would spontaneously ignite, restoring fire to the island.

If a priest were needed from the mainland to attend a dying islander, the sea would calm the moment his boat touched the water. There were separate

Above: A perfect specimen of a clochan or beehive hut on Inishmurray, showing the corbel-shaped roof of dry masonry.
Left: Cursing stones, Inishmurray. They were used to bring down maledictions on one's enemies.

cemeteries for men and for women; if one of the wrong sex were buried in the wrong cemetery the corpse would be supernaturally ejected by the desecrated grave, and projected to its own place in its proper cemetery. Inishmurray - not exactly the right place to be left behind after a day's trip!

Returning to the main Sligo-Bundoran road at Creevykeel crossroads, a sign-post stands a little way towards Bundoran, pointing out a 180 foot-long court cairn, otherwise known as the Creevykeel Giants' Graves. Excavated in 1935 by the Harvard archaeological expedition, the cairn yielded the remains of four cremated burials, as well as pottery and stone axes. As can be seen, the court leads into a gallery with two burial chambers.

THE VALLEYS OF GLENIFF, GLENADE AND GLENCAR

We now take the road towards the northern aspect of Ben Bulben, following the sign for Ballintrillick. From there we take the mountain road for Truskmore (2113 feet, the highest peak in County Sligo) the site of the RTE television transmitter built in 1962. We're now in the Gleniff Valley with its horseshoe road, a circular drive with panoramic views. The Gleniff caves are the finest in County Sligo. Impressively situated 1,200 feet up, and above a precipitous rock face of forty feet, there is an immense natural arch forty feet high and sixty feet wide. This is called Diarmuid and Gráinne's bed. There are stalactites and stalagmites in Gleniff cave 'in every fantastic form that nature can desire,' as Wood-Martin says. Near its opening there is a steeple-like pinnacle rearing itself over a precipice of about two hundred feet.

Legend says Gleniff cave is the last resting place of Diarmuid and Gráinne. For sixteen years they were pursued by the elderly and vengeful Fionn Mac Cumhail, to whom Gráinne had been betrothed. Overtly reconciled, Fionn invited Diarmuid to a hunt, tricking him into fighting an enchanted boar. The hunt ended on the slopes of Ben Bulben when Diarmuid was fatally injured by the boar. With water from a magical well cupped in his hands, Fionn could have saved his rival's life, but he refused to help. Instead, he sent Diarmuid's head to Gráinne who died on seeing it. They carried her from the Caves of Keshcorran (see Chapter 16) to Gleniff and laid her with Diarmuid.

We return through Ballintrillick, retracing the Creevykeel road for about a mile, and then turn right for Kinlough. Four miles ahead we join the Kinlough-Manorhamilton road, turning right to pass through the impressively scenic valley of Glenade, flanked on either side by the cliff-faced mountains of Sligo and Leitrim.

A plaque on a house in one of Manorhamilton's narrow streets reads: 'Office of Seán Mac Diarmada, General Election, 1908.' A signatory of the 1916 Proclamation, Mac Diarmuidhe was afterwards executed. Nearby Kilty-clogher was his birthplace. Built in 1638, the remains of Sir Frederick Hamil-

Creevykeel Cairn: an entrance passage through the east end (near the surrounding wall) leads to a court, off whose west end opens a two-chamber gallery grave.

ton's castle still dominate Manorhamilton. This was his base when he sacked Sligo in 1642, destroying its Abbey and slaughtering its people (see Chapter 3).

We now follow the Glencar valley road for about seven miles to reach the lake which, to be seen properly, must be circumnavigated. To do this we keep to the main road which rises parallel with the lake below. There is a viewing lay-by. Opposite is the Ben Bulben range of mountains where Alpine plants are to be found. Many waterfalls cascade from the cliff-tops, especially after rain, and, if the wind is in the right direction, they are lifted into the air, to burst into gem-like local rainbows if the sun is shining. The Irish name of one such

*Looking towards the Gleniff Valley and the Horse
Shoe Mountain road.*

waterfall translates as 'the stream against the height' because of its effect of
flowing upwards.

Straight ahead we take the first turn right leading down to the lakeside road.
Towering behind us is Lugnagall and 'the Protestant leap', the cliff over which
Hamilton's horsemen rode to their doom after sacking Sligo (see Chapter 3).
Yeats invokes the mountain in *'The Man Who Dreamed of Faeryland'*:

> He slept under the hill of Lugnagall;
> And might have known at last unhaunted sleep
> Under that cold and vapour-turbaned steep,
> Now that the earth had taken man and all:
> Did not the worms that spired about his bones
> Proclaim with that unwearied, reedy cry

*Situated between King's Mountain and Lugnagall Mountain, Glencar Lake
is shared by counties Sligo and Leitrim.*

That God has laid His fingers on the sky,
That from those fingers glittering summer runs
Upon the dancer by the dreamland wave.
Why should those lovers that no lovers miss
Dream, until God burn Nature with a kiss?
The man has found no comfort in the grave.

The lakeside road takes us past the old terminus for the cablecars which
brought down barytes (used in paint-making) from the Ben Bulben mines. A
narrow-gauge railway once brought the ore to Mullaghmore for export. At the
car park a sign on the left points to the waterfall. This is *the* Glencar Waterfall.
It is difficult to convey the sense of other-worldliness one experiences at this
most heavenly corner of County Sligo. I recommend that you memorise ten
lines of Yeats and repeat them to yourself as you linger in this misty, green and
faery-haunted place:

Where the wandering water gushes
From the hills above Glen-car,
In pools among the rushes
That scarce could bathe a star,

Siberry's Cottage in the Glencar Valley in the early 1900s.

We seek for slumbering trout
And whispering in their ears
Give them unquiet dreams;
Leaning softly out
From ferns that drop their tears
Over the young streams.

Once upon a time there was an entrancingly romantic cottage near the waterfall. Thatched with golden straw, it was called Siberry's, and as I remember it, they served afternoon tea on a close-cut lawn, with home-made scones and blackberry jam. That was long ago when food, glorious food, impressed an ever-hungry lad more than the glorious scenery that surrounded him. Siberry's had a visitors' book which would have been a collector's item for the great names it contained. Yeats was a frequent visitor, and in 1895 entertained Arthur Symonds, the Welsh poet, here for two weeks.

Of Sligo and its people Symonds said: 'How indeed is it possible that they should not see more of the other world than most folk do, and catch dreams in their nets? For it is a place of dreams, a grey, gentle place, where the sand melts into the sea, the sea into the sky, and the mountains and clouds drift into one another. I have never seen so friendly a sea nor a sea so full of the ecstasy of sleep.'

At the end of Glencar lake, to the left, a rough track through a wood leads into the Swiss Valley, a sheltered defile with a cliff of grey limestone on one side, and a slope covered with silver birches on the other. Alpine flora grow from the cliffs and arbutus in the valley.

Where the lakeside road joins the Sligo-Manorhamilton road we turn right, and once more, as we head for Sligo, we can look over Glencar with its guardian mountains, and see the tower of Drumcliff Church to the west of the valley, set off against the more distant waters of Sligo Bay.

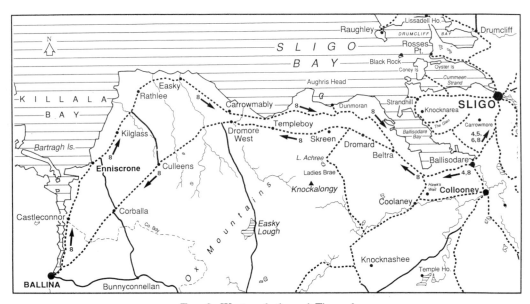

Tour 8 - Westwards through Tireragh

Chapter 19

Westwards through Tireragh

Our tour of west Sligo brings us once again through Ballisodare where, over the bridge, we turn right, following the Ballina road. We covered this road - in the opposite direction - on the return journey from our circuit of The Hawk's Well, Coolaney, 'The Drear Hart Lake' and the Ladies' Brae (see Chapter 15). Depending upon the ever-changing light, the east-west drive brings out more vividly the rugged beauty of the Ox Mountains, particularly in the early stages of our journey when they are close at hand. The further west we go, the further the mountains distance themselves.

Beyond the Beltra woods (in which stands Tanrego House, a Georgian mansion) there is a long, tedious hill, hardly noticeable to a motorist, but once a formidable proposition, in either direction, for a yoked horse. One dark night my father and mother were driving home in a back-to-back trap. Suddenly the horse stopped in its stride, stubbornly refusing to go on. It was accepted that horses could sense the presence of evil spirits, and not far away was a house reputed to be haunted by something particularly evil. My father got down to lead the horse, but still it refused to move. Unhitching a candle-lit lamp from the trap, he walked a few yards ahead. Something began to reflect the light. It was the brass mountings on a coffin. Knowing local customs better than my mother - now stiff with fright - he manhandled the obviously empty box on to the verge of the road. Resuming their journey, he assured my mother they'd soon come on the owner. They did. Further down the road a drunken carter was fast asleep on top of his load, while his horse made its own way home. He took unkindly to the idea of driving back a few miles for the lost property of a neighbour whom, he protested, he was only obliging by bringing the coffin from Sligo.

Incidentally, the goings-on in the haunted house - only one of dozens in the locality - were told and re-told with indecent relish by adults ignorant of the terror they were instilling into curious children. This particular ghost seemed to detest prayers and holy pictures - the framed variety. In this house at any hour of the day or night a holy picture could crash to the floor in smithereens. But it was when the household knelt to say their nightly rosary that their resentful lodger showed his real paces. Windows rattled, soot blew from the chimneys, chairs came crashing down the stairs, and something invisible

At mating time fearsome billy-goats come down from the Ox Mountains.

would spit real wet saliva into their faces. Gossip thrived. When not-so-sick patients called, bursting to tell the latest horror, my mother would say: 'Not in front of the children - please,' to which my father would add by way of explanation: 'Little pigs have big ears' - all of which annoyed me intensely, knowing I was being done out of something really blood-curdling. Eventually the bishop made a hush-hush visit to the house. What he did nobody seemed to know. It was something of a mystery. But whatever he did, he put an end to one of the spiciest stories of my haunted Sligo childhood.

THE WILD IRISH GIRL

Traversing the countryside between the Ox Mountains and the Atlantic we are traversing the Barony of Tireragh, stretching from Ballisodare to Ballina, the land of the chieftains O'Dowd until the ill-fated year of 1641 when, like so many of their compatriots, they met ruination. Longford House, the seat of the Crofton family, is built on the site of Longford Castle, an O'Dowd stronghold. It was at this house that Sydney Owenson, later Lady Morgan, wrote *The Wild Irish Girl*, the novel that made her the toast of Europe. Her actor father played regularly in the Sligo theatre, where the Theatre Royal

Hardy creatures, the black-faced sheep still suffer in winter when the Sligo mountains are often the first in the country to be covered in snow.

Company from Dublin's Crow Street were also frequent visitors. According to Wood-Martin, Owenson was considered good at 'impersonating the middle class of Paddies.' To reach Longford House and the Dromard holy well (see Chapter 2) we turn left at Skreen at a pub called 'The Fiddler's Elbow'.

Re-joining the main road, we shortly meet a fork with a telephone kiosk between the roads, and Skreen Garda Station to the left. We take the left-hand fork - not the road turning acutely left. In a few minutes we're in the old village of Skreen at the north end of the Red Hill which is 555 feet high, and has a large stone ring-fort on its summit. St Adamnan, the biographer of St Colmcille, built a church in Skreen in the seventh century. Over the copiously-flowing Adamnan's well, on the right of the road, stands a monument bearing a Latin inscription, which, translated, reads: 'Eugene Mc Donnell, Vicar of this district had me erected, 1591.' Neglect has allowed the growth of a tree whose roots now disturb the foundation of this unique monument.

Built in 1818, the Church of Ireland overlooks a ruined abbey and an old cemetery containing some very beautiful stonework, done mostly by generations of local sculptors, the Diamond family. Skreen's most famous parson was the Reverend Edward Nangle, alias 'The Great Nangle', formerly the notorious proselytiser of the Achill Island Mission (see Chapter 5). In his book, *The Windings of the Moy*, the Reverend James Greer writes charmingly of Nangle who founded the Skreen Teachers' Training School, situated further up the hill. As a pupil in 1863, newly arrived by Bianconi car, Greer's pen-picture of Nangle is of a kindly, compassionate man who believed implicitly in his life's mission, and allowed nothing to stand in the way of its accomplishment.

Moving on, the old Skreen road re-joins the main road where we turn left. The four miles to Dromore West cover elevated ground from which there are magnificent views of Ben Bulben and Knocknarea, and over Sligo and Donegal bays. At Dunflin there is a monument - sadly neglected - marking the site of the inn where Duald Mac Firbis, the last historiographer of the O'Dowds of Tireragh, was murdered by the buck, Thomas Crofton in 1671 (see Chapter 1). At Grange Beg we pass near the house where I spent my impressionable childhood. On the hill behind it, somewhere now hidden by the trees, is the rath where one boy's dreams were made. Given to sentimentality, I must be firm and always keep moving through this countryside. To linger might be to shatter for ever some of my most cherished dreams.

The approach to Dromore West shows a prettily situated village. On the left once stood the barracks of the Royal Irish Constabulary (see Chapter 8). Above the waterfall was the site of Dunneill Castle, another O'Dowd stronghold, where Hugh Roe O'Donnell spent his last Christmas in Ireland. Also overlooking the Dunneill waterfall was Miss Lougheed's house. A patient of my father's, she kept aristocratic goats with floppy ears, as well as black-and-white rabbits and Belgian hares. The women of the area owed her much. She opened a coffee shop on the green for the monthly cattle fair, not for any profit motive, but to facilitate men who might otherwise roll home 'paralatic' to their wives, victims of the less scrupulous publicans.

BALLINA TO ENNISCRONE

Leaving the village we take the left fork for Ballina. In a moment we pass the fair green where once a year the Big Top of Duffy's Circus lent the place a badly-needed air of festivity. Another mile brings us to the old Dromore West Workhouse where I often went with my father. I remember it more for luxury than for the crude and terrible poverty of the unfortunate occupants of its wards. The institution - burnt out in the Troubles - stood on the edge of a vast heather-covered bog. The matron had a taste for heather-honey and provided scrumptious, never-to-be-forgotten teas. I tucked in with a boy's appetite and an equally boyish inability to recognise the difference between luxury and deprivation side-by-side.

Crossing the river Easky we emerge on to the wide open spaces of the Culleens Bog, where the air is always fresh, and sometimes heather-scented. We are following the Mail Coach Road, purpose-built in the last century. It is the best road in County Sligo. Away to the south-west, on the far side of Lough Conn, can be seen the sugar-loafed shape of Mount Nephin rearing itself nearly 2,700 feet from the Lahardaun countryside. We are about to over-run the western boundary of County Sligo by some four miles to reach Ballina, County Mayo. Our intrusion is for the purpose of gaining access to the scenic Quay Road by which we will return along the river Moy and the coast.

Meantime we note the imposing and picturesque approach to Ballina, its most impressive feature being, of course, the river Moy. The Bunree river, tumbling over its rapids past the Downhill Hotel, joins the Moy at the Sligo road. Further along on the left is the old Episcopal Palace, then comes St Muredach's College, and then, dominating everything, the Cathedral, designed by Sir John Benson, a County Sligo man (see Chapter 16). It was built in the late 1820s, beside the ruins of a fourteenth century Augustinian Priory, at a time of great poverty for the Roman Catholic Church. But Ballina Cathedral came into existence largely through work done voluntarily by builders, masons, carpenters and carters. It is interesting that this generous response was inspired by a young man called Father John McHale. Later he severed his priestly connection with Killala Diocese to become a distinguished Archbishop of Tuam. It will be remembered that he was the little boy who, in 1798, stood in a flax field at Lahardaun and watched Humbert's blue-coated infantry pass on their way from Killala to Castlebar (see Chapter 4). The Ardnaree Church of Ireland, further along near the second bridge, was built in 1768, that is, thirty years before Humbert's force passed that way.

Leaving Ballina we follow the right bank of the Moy by turning left beyond the Bunree Bridge to reach the Quay Road. On the opposite side is the well-situated Belleek Manor, once Belleek House, and, once again, Ballina House. Through Crocketstown past the Ballina Quays and about three miles ahead, at Castleconnor, we re-enter County Sligo. Here on the banks of the Moy, where the river widens, stand the ruins of Castle Connor, once the principal stronghold of the O'Dowds, for centuries the lords of Tireragh. Dispossessed during the Cromwellian confiscations between 1621 and 1642, the lands and castle passed to a planter of Coote's Regiment serving under Cromwell.

The spire of Killanly Church of Ireland - untypically for a Protestant church - is surmounted by a cross. Colonel Wingfield, a man strong and narrow in religious and political opinions, and a veteran of Waterloo, lived grandly at nearby Moyview. He rode up daily to monitor the progress of the building of

Enniscrone Castle, once a stronghold of the O'Dowds, with the ruins
of Valentine's Church, so called because a Parson Valentine was a
one-time incumbent. Enniscrone has spread since
W.F. Wakeman made this drawing in 1879.

the church in 1827. He had promised a celebration on the completion of the
spire. One day he arrived to find the scaffolding down, and the workmen
standing about admiring the final touch - the cross on the pinnacle. The Colonel
became enraged and sent for the parson who, truthfully, pleaded ignorance. A
craftsman had earlier fallen to his death from the scaffolding. So now, not even
Colonel Wingfield's most generous blandishments would encourage a man-
jack of them back up that steeple to remove the cross - so there it remains.

Opposite Killanly on the far side of the river stands Rosserk Abbey, a
fifteenth century foundation, said to be 'the best preserved Franciscan Tertiary
friary in Ireland.' A mile down-river, opposite Bartragh Island, is Moyne
Abbey, another near-perfect Franciscan foundation dating from 1462, and
needing only to be re-roofed. Both abbeys were attacked and burned in 1590.
Both are worthy of a visit. The cloister at Moyne is superb, and the view from
the top of the tower is well worth the climb.

A mile or two ahead is Scurmore, the site of the Seven Children of the
Mermaid. The story concerns an O'Dowd of Tireragh who came upon a
mermaid clad in a magnificent mantle and sleeping by the sea. He took the
mantle and hid it, thereby removing the maid's power to return to the sea. Then
he married her, and they had seven children. One day the youngest saw his
father moving this gorgeous mantle to a safer hiding place. He told his mother.
She recovered her mantle, but before escaping back to the sea, she revenged

herself by magically changing her children into seven rocks, which, according to local legend, still bleed every seven years.

A little nearer Enniscrone is Muckduff, or the Valley of the Black Pig, which has its own legend. A monstrous wild boar appeared in County Donegal where it devoured children and attacked men and women. It was pursued south into County Sligo where, cornered, it took to the sea. Making its landfall on Enniscrone beach, it floundered up the Bellawaddy river where it was finally slain and buried. A mound marks its grave.

Noted for its sunsets, Enniscrone's greatest attraction must be its three-mile beach, safe in all weathers, and extending westwards to where the Moy enters the sea. William and Elizabeth Pollexfen used to holiday here, sometimes joined by their daughter, Susan Yeats and her children. In fact, it was here that Willie's elder sister, Susan Mary (Lily) was born in 1866 while Mrs Yeats was on a visit to her parents.

The land of my fathers, they are commemorated in a stained glass window in Enniscrone parish church. Once a triptych window over the high altar in the old church, it was transferred in the 1950s. Adapted for its new surroundings, it is now on the right side of the chancel of the modern church.

Leaving Enniscrone we pass another ruined castle of the O'Dowds, and then through Cowells' Cross, a crossroads so called because the family owned the surrounding lands.

KILGLASS AND DUALD MACFIRBIS

Two miles ahead, at Kilglass Church of Ireland, a deviation to the right leads almost immediately to the old Abbey of Kilglass. Here the Cowell family vault overlooks the road. Kilglass is the reputed burial place of Duald MacFirbis. The hereditary historians of the O'Dowds, Chieftains of Tireragh, the MacFirbis family lived at Castle Lecan, Kilglass, a centre of Gaelic scholarship from the thirteenth to the seventeenth century. Nothing remains of the castle, but a plaque marks the site.

The last of the line, Duald compiled the *Book of the Genealogies of Ireland*, containing the history of Irish and anglo-Irish families. It is now in the library of University College, Dublin. *The Book of Lecan*, now in the Royal Irish Academy, and *The Yellow Book of Lecan*, now in Trinity College, were compiled by, or under the direction of, members of the MacFirbis family at Lecan. These, with *The Book of Ballymote* and the *O'Gara Manuscript*, both in the Royal Irish Academy, make up a distinguished historical contribution from County Sligo to the national archives.

The Reverend James Greer, author of *The Windings of the Moy*, made his own contribution. Armed with a blackthorn stick and a little Gladstone bag, he wandered the countryside collecting historical material for articles he

Fionn Mac Cumhaill's Split Rock on the Easky-Dromore West road.

published in *The Western People* newspaper. He was a frequent visitor to our house. He never left without ceremoniously replenishing his hip-flask from the decanter. Looking back, he was more like an ancient Irish bard than a retired reverend.

THE SEA ROAD TO SLIGO

Returning to the main road, we continue through Rathlee and Easky, beyond which, on the right, is the Split Rock. The legend is that Fionn Mac Cumhail in a temper threw it from the mountain, intending it for the sea. It fell short, worsening his temper, so he then split it with his sword. You may go through it twice, but not three times or it will close on you. I have gone through a third time, not without feeling a certain sense of desecrating centuries of legend. The coldly unimaginative explain the rock as an Ice Age erratic.

Instead of going through Dromore West, we keep straight, to follow the sea road. I have already written about the view from Carrowmably Martello tower - our Castle of Dromore (see Chapter 2). It is near the new water tower at Dromore West and is well worth a visit. Two miles ahead there is a left turn for Aughris Head, a prominent feature on the County Sligo coastline, its sheer cliffs rising two hundred feet out of the Atlantic, generating a terror out of all proportion to their height. From his priory here, St Molaise converted the pagans of Inishmurray Island. I remember Aughris village as a street of closely-set thatched cottages, sheltered from the north winds behind the peak of the promontory. Now it is a tumbled, deserted village.

Maurteen Bruin in *The Land of Heart's Desire* produces some 'precious wine' to entertain Father Hart. Telling how he came by it Maurteen says: 'There was a Spaniard wrecked at Ocris Head, when I was young, and I have still some bottles'. Yeats often took peculiar liberties with placenames, like Ocris for Aughris and Cro Patric for Croagh Patrick, as if he had tried to spell them phonetically because he had never seen them written down.

An interesting feature of Aughris Head is the Coragh dTonn, a narrow chasm opening high over a cave which penetrates - nobody knows how far - into the cliffs. When the sea-swell enters the cave, it compresses the air within until it is forcibly released with a loud explosion. The noise can be heard many miles away, even at the far side of the Ox Mountains, and even in calm weather. Cut into the rock at the top of the chasm are the imprints of a horse's hooves. Somebody once told me that Countess Markievicz had jumped her horse over this yawning obstacle, leaving the hoof-marks.

An alternative explanation is recorded by Wood-Martin, and is said to have been told to tourists by the driver of a Bianconi car plying between Sligo and Ballina: 'There was no place in all the world where Alexander the Great wasn't able to ride his horse, till he came to Aughris. There he galloped his horse up to the very edge of the cliff, but when the beast saw the waves raging below, he reared up on his hind legs, and stopped short. The two marks of his hoofs are there still to be seen. I have seen them myself! What better evidence can be required?'

Sydney Owenson (Lady Morgan) wrote her *Lay of an Ancient Irish Harp* at Longford House. One poem in this book is inspired by Aughris Head and the Coragh dTonn:

> And the world's greatest ocean still dashes its wave
> 'Gainst the coast that is savagely wild:
> 'Midst the castle's grey ruins there still yawns a cave
> Where the sun's cheering light never smil'd.
> And steep is the precipice, horrid to view,
> That rears o'er the ocean its crest
> They say that no bird to its summit e'er flew,
> And its base 'neath the wave seems to rest.

Just east of Aughris is Dunmoran Beach, overlooked by another deserted village. In our time they held horse races here. Standing on a Guinness barrel, his field-glasses poised, my father was judge. Here I saw everything that Jack Yeats put into his early drawings of Sligo: the low tents on their bent poles, each flying a bedraggled tricolour; fortune tellers wearing heavy earrings and shawlies selling dilisk, the edible seaweed; wild-looking jockeys in their everyday clothes, their only gesture to the occasion being to turn their cloth caps back to front; and of course, the 'wide boys' out from Sligo on their spring-carts, ready to turn a penny, honest or otherwise. 'Caards o' the raacin', raacin' caards,' they called as they moved through a gathering more interested in counting their takings than in reading the pedigrees of horses already known to everybody.

Apart from that occasional jamboree, Dunmoran belonged to the seagulls. Now it has been discovered by Continental caravanners - and good luck to them. Nowhere else in the world will they find a place so permeated with that clean scent of seaweed that never fails to improve one's sense of well-being.

Before we re-join the main road, entering the woods at Tanrego, we get some dramatic views of Knocknarea across Ballisodare Bay. Our return to Sligo is, of course, through Ballisodare.

Epilogue

'By His Command'

'Under bare Ben Bulben's head
In Drumcliff churchyard Yeats is laid.'

Monk Gibbon, the writer, was Yeats' cousin. They had a love-hate relationship. In 1965 Gibbon said: 'The Yeats band-waggon is overcrowded. Research students of every nationality spring up almost daily, thesis in hand. But those who knew Yeats personally are a diminishing body, and the longer one lives the greater one's rarity value becomes.' Now the time is coming when the same might be said of those who saw Yeats laid to rest in Drumcliff. I am one. The memory of it transcends all others of my adult memories of Sligo. We who worshipped from afar remembered back nine years to a January morning when

Radio Éireann (as it then was) broke the news of the poet's death. Stunned, we turned to the BBC for confirmation, only to find the English claiming him as their own. He had been out of Ireland for some time.

It was towards the end of 1938 that, for health reasons, Yeats went to Cap Martin in the Alpes Maritimes. Feeling, perhaps, the nearness of death, he wrote to a friend: 'It seems to me that I have found what I wanted. When I try to put all into a phrase, I say, "Man can embody truth but he cannot know it."' A week before his death on 28 January 1939, he said to his wife: 'If I die here bury me there on the mountain [the little steeply-terraced mountain cemetery at Roquebrune], and then after a year or so dig me up and bring me privately to Sligo.' Fate, in the terrible shape of World War II, intervened, and instead of one year, the poet lay for nine years in a French grave, until Seán MacBride, then Minister for External Affairs, moved to have him repatriated.

A POET'S HOMECOMING

It followed that early on a September morning in 1948, led by a cross-bearer and a priest, Yeats' coffin was carried down the hill to Cap Martin. Though the Anglican service was read at his graveside in 1939, he was now given a Catholic blessing, with even a sprinkling of holy water. He wouldn't have minded, for he it was who said: 'Christianity and the old nature faith have lain down side by side in the cottages, and I would proclaim that peace as loudly as I can among the kingdoms of poetry, where there is no peace that is not joyous, no battle that does not give life instead of death...'

Preceded by a French military band with muffled drums, the hearse arrived at Nice where a French bearer-party handed over to the Irish ratings who piped the poet's coffin aboard the corvette *Macha*. Within ten minutes she was putting out to sea, while a young priest pushed through the crowd to make the sign of the cross after her. The journey from the sunshine of southern France to the mists of north-west Ireland took eleven days. During that time Dublin, Galway and Sligo wrangled over the protocol of a poet's homecoming.

Dublin, the Irish Government and the press wanted a State funeral in the capital, as the coffin passed on its way to Sligo. The Dean of St Patrick's went further: he offered the honour of a grave within the cathedral near Swift and Stella - it would have been the first such burial for one hundred years. But in conformity with the poet's wishes, his family wanted a simple country funeral at Drumcliff. There had to be compromise. While Sligo waited for the arrival of the *Macha*, an announcement said she would berth instead in Galway where facilities were better. Indignation boiled in Sligo. Bigger ships had berthed there. Besides, the coffin could be taken ashore at the deep water quay at Elsinore in Rosses Point, William Middleton's summer home where Yeats had so often spent boyhood holidays. No good. Officialdom had its way. The

184

Right: Yeats' coffin is blessed at Roquebrune, France.
Below: Irish sailors receive the coffin from the French army.

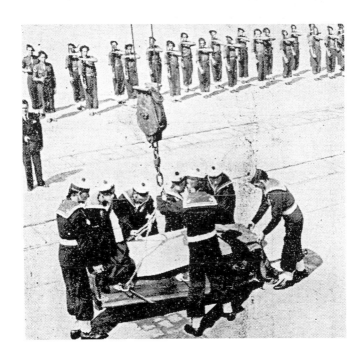

The funeral through O'Connell Street, Sligo.

Macha berthed in Galway.

Frank O'Connor welcomed his friend: 'The return of Yeats' remains to Ireland is an occasion for celebration. If they had come home nine years ago, we should probably have been thinking of our loss rather than of his achievement. Today we can think of his return only as the completion of a work long-planned, the crowning of a life which was like a great work of art, nobly conceived, nobly executed, and now brought to a triumphant conclusion. For it was part of the work of art as he saw it that he who took his inspiration from the landscape and people of Sligo should return to them in the end.'

After its ninety-mile journey from Galway, the cortège stopped at Sligo's Borough Boundary where it was met by the Mayor and members of the corporation and the county council. The Mayor, Councillor Michael Rooney, said: 'On behalf of the people of Sligo I pay this sincere tribute to the memory of one whose genius was inspired by the lakes and mountains of our countryside, and whose poetry has given the name of Sligo a place in the literature of the world - William Butler Yeats.'

186

*At the Yeats funeral (left to right): Dr Robert Collis, poet
Austin Clarke, John Cowell, poet Louis Mac Neice.*

Preceded by pipes and muffled drums, moving past the blinded shop-windows of Sligo, the hearse arrived before the City Hall to be greeted by the General Salute, sounded by a military bugler. A guard of honour was drawn up, soldiers with bowed heads and reversed arms taking their places round the hearse - 'four tired soldiers', as the misunderstanding 'Pope' O'Mahony called them in a radio interview. The coffin - covered with a Tricolour and a laurel wreath - wasn't removed from the hearse during the two-hour lying-in-state - a convenient break for admirers from afar to refresh themselves.

Early that morning in Dublin I had collected my little party for the drive to Sligo: Austin Clarke, Ernie O'Malley, Mary Andrews and my sister, Vera. The further west we went, the thicker became the mist. By the time we had reached County Sligo, Ben Bulben was hidden, gone into mourning, with only the pattern of the stone-walled fields at its base emerging from the mist into the light. Under leaden skies, it was a soft Irish day, and who would have had it otherwise? Anything else would have been inappropriate for the poet's home-coming.

'Where Ben Bulben mixes into the sea wind,' they laid him in a fern-lined grave, and slowly they shovelled the Drumcliff earth over him. And when the grave-diggers moved back, the Mayor of Sligo moved forward: 'Today we have fulfilled the expressed desires of W.B. Yeats,' he said, 'that he might rest in the shelter of Ben Bulben, and that his homecoming might be marked by the least ceremony. Simplicity was the keynote of his wishes. Faithfulness has been the watchword of our efforts to accomplish their fulfilment. Speaking on behalf of the Yeats family and the people of Sligo, I desire to thank those who have gathered today to do honour to his memory. Let the epitaph of W.B. Yeats now be inscribed on stone - "Cast a cold eye on life, on death. Horseman, pass by."'

Drumcliff churchyard had never seen so many and such cheerful mourners, for Yeats had been dead for nine years. Despite the weather, there was a festive air. Lennox Robinson was merry, and Edward Longford sported a red carnation. There was a sense of relief, of triumph, in having our greatest poet home again, and safely bestowed in the place he had designated for himself. Little could he have dreamt of his future debt to MacBride when he wrote from Normandy to Lady Gregory in 1920 that he had 'imagined he did not like little boys, but that he found he did like little Seán MacBride.' It was as the most internationally recognised Minister for External Affairs Ireland ever had that Seán MacBride represented the Irish Government at Yeats' last journey. His mother, Maud Gonne, remained at home in Roebuck too frail to attend the burial of the man who had once loved the 'pilgrim soul' in her and the sorrows of her 'changing face'.

As evening closed in, and the rain still fell incessantly, we, 'the indomitable Irishry', went our various roads. Wayside wakes were held in hostelries in Carrick and Longford, in Mullingar and Kinnegad. Willie Yeats was analysed, his work dissected, but not even the hated philistines, his meanest begrudgers, could deny that his life had been without artistic precedent in Ireland. To say that Yeats' legacy to Sligo, to Ireland, to the world, is incalculable would be grossly to understate. As long as English literature is read, so long will men and women revel in the occult, the spiritual, the essence of ancient Ireland, those magical elements out of which Yeats compounded his poetry.

Susan Pollexfen Yeats, his mother, was never given the recognition she deserved for inculcating the sense of magic inherent in the Sligo lore she passed on to her children. Even in far-away London she managed to sustain the idea that Sligo was a more desirable place than any other in the world.

What would have pleased and probably surprised Willie Yeats is the universal acceptance of his work. He hoped he might be read and appreciated

Yeats' final resting place - Drumcliff churchyard.

by the Irish people, especially those of his beloved Sligo. But he could never have foreseen an annual Yeats International Summer School in that city, with scholars coming from the four corners of the world to elucidate, to analyse, to argue over his stanzas, his hidden symbols, his secret emotions. He'd surely have enjoyed it all:

> I celebrate the silent kiss that ends short life and long.
> Never to have lived is best, ancient writers say;
> Never to have drawn the breath of life, never to have looked into
>   the eye of day;
> The second best's a gay goodnight and quickly turn away.

189

Index